houseplant
warrior

houseplant warrior

7 KEYS TO UNLOCKING THE MYSTERIES OF HOUSEPLANT CARE

RAFFAELE DI LALLO

CREATOR OF OHIO TROPICS

The Countryman Press

An Imprint of W. W. Norton & Company
Independent Publishers Since 1923

Copyright © 2022 by Raffaele Di Lallo
Foreword copyright © 2022 by Gretchen Mason

For information about permission to reproduce selections from this book, write to
Permissions, The Countryman Press, 500 Fifth Avenue, New York, NY 10110

For information about special discounts for bulk purchases, please contact
W. W. Norton Special Sales at specialsales@wwnorton.com or 800-233-4830

Manufacturing by Versa Press
Book design by Allison Chi
Production managers: Gwen Cullen and Devon Zahn

The Countryman Press
www.countrymanpress.com

A division of W. W. Norton & Company, Inc.
500 Fifth Avenue, New York, NY 10110
www.wwnorton.com

978-1-68268-675-1

10 9 8 7 6 5 4 3 2 1

This book is primarily dedicated to my husband, David, who has been the biggest supporter of my Ohio Tropics endeavor and has tolerated the constant influx and outflux of plants throughout the years, both indoors and outdoors. Without his support, it would be very difficult to be where I am today. I would just ask him to reconsider allowing me to place plants in the beautiful, sunny southern window in our home. Of course, if it would result in divorce, I suppose I could forego this prospect.

I also dedicate this book to my loyal followers and readers, many of whom have stuck with me from the beginning and have provided the spark and encouragement to keep me going. Without you this book would not be possible, so thank you for helping me grow on this journey with you.

contents

foreword

I'm honored to have been asked to write this foreword for Raffaele Di Lallo, my good friend and colleague in the plant community. Raffaele and I first met years ago through our alter egos, @ohiotropics and @greenhousegirl94, on Instagram. I was immediately impressed by his large collection of plants, which includes both trendy, more difficult to obtain tropicals and more traditional houseplants, some exceeding 10 years in age, which I refer to as Heirloom Plants. Raffaele's plants are evidence that he's been collecting plants for a very long time and is exceptionally adept at plant care.

Over the course of getting to know each other, Raffaele and I soon realized we have the "same brain," as we call it, when it comes to plant care practices and our mutual desire to educate others on how to care for their plants.

Aside from having an incredible collection of houseplants, Raffaele has a wealth of plant care knowledge that he loves to share with others. He's gifted at breaking down information that may be overwhelming into easy-to-understand teachings. From photosynthesis to phototropism, Raffaele covers it all by using simple language and practical examples.

Interest in houseplants is at an all-time high, and I regularly use Raffaele's tutorials and writings to help educate myself as well as my customers on a variety of plant subjects. I routinely recommend Raffaele's first two books and his blogs on plant care to my customers in the large, tropical greenhouse where I work.

I truly value my friendship with Raffaele, and I respect both his incredible knowledge of houseplants and his willingness to share it with others. I'm confident that plant novices as well as experienced plant collectors will benefit from the invaluable information that Raffaele so generously shares here.

GRETCHEN MASON
Merrifield Garden Center
(Fairfax, Virginia)

Jewel Orchid (*Ludisia discolor*) cutting

introduction

My houseplant obsession started very early in life. As a child, I had read somewhere that houseplants could clean the air. Growing up, I was disgusted with my father's two-pack-a-day smoking habit, so I started amassing quite a few houseplants in elementary school and high school to counteract this.

As the product of an Italian immigrant family, growing plants is in my blood. From fig trees, oleanders, geraniums, and huge vegetable gardens outdoors, to an assortment of houseplants and endless cuttings indoors, plants have been a part of my life for as long as I can remember. I started growing houseplants long before the current rage. I would imagine that most people in elementary school are not interested in growing houseplants, but that's exactly when my lifelong passion began.

Although I went on to study chemical engineering in college, my career did eventually come full circle back to plants. As it turned out, my analytical and problem-solving background helped me help others with houseplant care. It all started with a phone call from my friend Donna when she confidently announced that I should share my knowledge and start a blog to help people out with their plants. The next day, in typical Raffaele fashion when I get overly excited about something, my website and Instagram (@ohiotropics), were born.

My engineering curriculum refined my critical thinking skills and fostered my observation-based approach to plant care. I *verify* what is actually happening with struggling plants. Too often, plant parents take the advice they receive at face value. For example, they may read somewhere that "overwatering causes yellow leaves" without actually verifying the truth of that advice for their particular circumstance. Perhaps instead they should observe the state of their potting mix. The truth is that yellow leaves can be caused by myriad factors. Ultimately, as a plant parent it is up to you to determine what is happening. Did you actually feel your potting mix to see if it was wet? This can cause yellow leaves. Or perhaps your potting mix was in fact very dry. This can also cause yellow leaves. You won't know unless you physically observe it! In order to be a successful plant parent, you must be able to employ critical thinking and questioning skills, and make astute observations about your plants.

No one is born with a green thumb. Whether it is intentional or not, we've all killed a plant or two . . . or three. But with each failure comes a lesson! After 30-plus years of growing houseplants and developing a proverbial green thumb, I've

White Moth Orchid (*Phalaenopsis*)

encountered many terrible misconceptions and myths that are hindering generations, young and old, from being able to have thriving houseplants.

From all the questions that I've fielded from my blog readers and Instagram and YouTube followers, as well as from my houseplant consultation clients, I've heard it all. I've received many frantic messages,

comments, and e-mails from helpless plant parents begging me to save their dying plants. The most common plea is perhaps, "Help, my plant is dying!" Oftentimes, once I ask the plant parent in question to supply me with a photo of their "dying" plant, I'm amused to find out that only the smallest, very oldest leaf has turned yellow and the rest of the plant looked as healthy as can be. No leaf lasts forever. Conversely, many times it is not a false alarm and I see evidence of a plant that truly is in distress. Some other common pleas for help include: "Why is my plant not growing?" "Why are my leaves turning brown and crispy?" "I want my plants to look like yours! What can I do?" "I received a peace lily from my father's funeral and it's not looking good. How can I save it?"

My main goal for you, the reader, is that you learn how to look at plant care holistically and also learn how to *question* your approaches and methods. Many plant parents get stuck on one aspect of care, such as watering or light. They think drooping branches and browning leaves are the results of *one* mistake. For these plant parents, perhaps overwatering or a lack of sun immediately come to mind. But in order to grow spectacularly thriving plants, you have to consider a variety of factors: light, water, fertilizer, soil, humidity, temperature, pot type and size, and *consistency* in care.

Successful plant care results from viewing all of these aforementioned topics holistically. This is why plant care is often confusing and frustrating for many. There is rarely a one-size-fits-all approach to plant care. For example, let's say that your friend tells you that she has had success with watering a particular houseplant once a week. You cannot safely take this advice because your conditions are likely different. Perhaps your indoor environment is warmer, your plant is in a much smaller pot, has a coarser potting mix, or has much more light than your friend's. All of these factors will cause your potting mix to dry

out much more quickly, and thus the plant requires more frequent watering. I go into the tricky topic of watering schedules later in this book.

To add to all of this, patience is also required! In this digital age where so much information is instantly available at our fingertips, our patience is thin and we demand answers immediately. In contrast, nature teaches us patience.

It's time to rewind, slow down, and go back to the basics—patience will be instrumental in your houseplant care journey. Because plant care really is a *journey* and not a destination, there will always be trial and error. I want to help you foster a deeper appreciation for nature, and along the way learn to pause instead of panic. Stopping to ask the right questions, to observe, to problem-solve, is so critical for success.

Questioning is key to problem-solving. Einstein once said: "If I had an hour to solve a problem and my life depended on the solution, I would spend the first 55 minutes determining the proper question to ask . . . for once I know the proper question, I could solve the problem in less than five minutes."

It is through my education as an engineer and problem solver that I have been able to ask my readers and clients the right questions. And it is my hope that I can educate you, the readers of this book, to learn how to ask the right questions. It is time to *empower* yourself!

I'll also teach you how to observe. So many times, when people have a plant problem, they simply jump to conclusions. They might cry out something like, "My peace lily has completely wilted, so I must have overwatered!" But then they fail to actually observe their own plant. Of course, when I ask them to actually feel the soil, they're shocked to find that it is completely dry.

Assumptions, myths, and lack of observation are detrimental in your houseplant care journey. It is time to be a more *mindful plant parent*. In today's modern society, mindfulness is needed more than ever. Many of us are routinely rushing from one activity to another and lead very busy lives, so it is only human nature to pursue the path of least resistance when we have a plant problem. This often results in a quick Google search to find the answer. Many will blindly accept the results of freshly queried information, which is often either grossly oversimplified or just flat out incorrect, without any consideration of the credibility of the source. This often results in "fixing" the wrong thing, which in turn creates worse issues and perpetuates a cycle of doom. In the end, the plant parent is left with even more confusion and less confidence.

Finally, I'd like to touch on the effect of social media on houseplants. The global reach of social media is staggering, and it has helped to spread the love of plants, and drive plant sales, like wildfire. This is a great thing! As a result, there are countless Facebook groups, Instagram profiles, and YouTube accounts devoted to plant care that give a lot of conflicting information. Furthermore, photos in social media are often misleading. Perfectly coiffed and immaculately staged and styled plants, although inspirational, have created unrealistic expectations and many misconceptions in houseplant care that are continually reinforced online. As a result, this has made it very confusing for the masses, particularly for those new to growing houseplants. It is great to be inspired, but as plant parents, we need to look beyond the conflicting advice and sleek photos and understand what we need to do to help our houseplants thrive.

That's where I step in. I've got you. I understand your frustration. I know why you're confused, and you deserve to have good information that will help you on your journey. If you read and absorb this entire book from cover to cover, you will have a solid foundation in houseplant care and set yourself on the path to becoming the confident plant parent you've always wanted to be but never knew *how* to be.

Once you learn the fundamentals of houseplant care using a holistic approach, and learn how to conduct your own problem-solving, you can finally have the green thumb you've always wanted. Everyone's lifestyle and indoor conditions are different, so it is up to you to determine what works best for you!

Most important, don't forget to have patience with yourself and make lots of observations. Remember, it is a journey and not a destination, so be kind to yourself along the way. We all learn from our mistakes.

"The important thing is not to stop questioning."

—ALBERT EINSTEIN

PART ONE

Which Plant Is Right for You?

There are so many things to consider when choosing which houseplants to grow indoors. Whether you are just starting out or expanding your collection, all the choices out there make for an exciting but sometimes daunting task!

It is important to keep in mind that there is no such thing as a "houseplant," as all plants evolved outdoors. What we know as houseplants are the ones that are most well-suited to growing indoors. Some plants just simply aren't built to survive an indoor environment.

I like to think of it this way: when we bring plants indoors, as their caretakers and adoptive plant parents, we are taking the place of Mother Nature and it is up to us to provide them with everything they need in order to thrive in our indoor habitat.

Throughout this book, I pose many questions that you need to answer for yourself regarding your particular indoor habitat. But the first should always be about your environment.

Although it is tempting to obtain any plant that strikes our fancy, it's important not to give in to impulse. There are many important questions to ask ourselves first in order to best choose which plants will thrive under our conditions. When you put forethought into plant care, you set up yourself, and your plants, for success. Before purchasing a plant, think about your habitat and which plants will be best suited to your space:

- What kind of lifestyle do you lead? Are you home a lot or are you frequently absent? Some houseplants can tolerate neglect very well, and others will seemingly shrivel away at the utter mention of neglect.
- What is the natural light situation in your home? What size and exposure are your windows (north, south, east, west)? Do your windows have any obstructions from outdoors that limit light? Do you have any direct sun coming indoors? Houseplants run the gamut in terms of light requirements, and it is important to know if you can supply enough light, whether by natural or artificial means.
- What is the typical temperature and humidity level inside your home? Many plants tolerate a wide range in temperature and humidity, and some don't. These can be important considerations when choosing plants.
- Are you new to growing houseplants, or have you tried growing plants multiple times but failed? Although it may be tempting to grow more exotic, rare plants, it is best to start by becoming comfortable with easier-to-grow and commonly available plants. This will help you gain some necessary skills and confidence before you venture into growing something more hard-to-find and exotic.

RIGHT: Chinese Money Plant (*Pilea peperomioides*)

Key 1.

What Is the Light Like in My Environment?

Light is *the* most important topic in houseplant care. All plants need light for photosynthesis, which is a process by which they make their own food. In very simplified terms, in order for photosynthesis to occur, plants need carbon dioxide, water, and light to make sugars (plant food). We *need* plants in order to live because they release a lovely by-product: life-giving oxygen.

It is important to be aware of your light conditions in your indoor habitat when choosing which plants you want to grow. If you don't provide enough light for your plants, you are literally starving them. Would you ever adopt a baby and not feed it? This is exactly what would be happening if you place your plant in a dark corner.

If you neglect to provide enough light, it will make every other aspect of plant care very challenging and you can easily get caught in a vicious circle of plant perils.

You should select houseplants to grow based on your light conditions, and not the other way around. If you force a plant to grow in conditions that it doesn't like, you will not achieve good results, because fighting against nature is a losing battle.

For example, if you don't have any direct sun at all coming through your windows, growing succulents and cacti probably won't be a good idea. They will still grow, but they may not look like you expect. In fact, in such conditions many succulents will experience what is called etiolation. This simply means that the plant has stretched out. Most often this occurs when the plant doesn't get enough light. These types of plants need as much direct sun as they can get indoors or they won't be happy. Of course, you could supplement with grow lights if natural light is not abundant in your home.

Light is one of the most misunderstood and nebulous topics in houseplant care. Here are some things to consider.

WINDOW EXPOSURES

Understanding the type of light that typically comes in through different window exposures is a very helpful place to start when you're evaluating light in your home.

For unobstructed windows, southern-exposure windows have the brightest light and plenty of direct sun, and northern windows will have no direct sun and the least amount of light . . . if you live in the Northern Hemisphere!

If you live in the Southern Hemisphere, north and south will be reversed and northern windows will have the most light with plenty of direct sun, and southern windows will have the least amount of light and no direct sun.

Southern windows in the Northern Hemisphere (or northern windows if you live in the Southern Hemisphere) are ideal for sun-loving plants like string of pearls, ponytail palm, hibiscus, jade plants, bird-of-paradise, various cacti, among many others. These windows are a blessing to have because you can also diffuse the light with sheer curtains or partially closed blinds, meaning that you are able to grow a wider variety of plants. It is much easier to decrease the amount of light than to increase it!

Unobstructed eastern windows, regardless of where you live in the world, will have direct morning sun but then will receive indirect light the rest of the day. Conversely, western windows will have

Monstera deliciosa and *Ficus elastica*

afternoon direct sun, which is more intense and hotter than the gentler morning sun coming through eastern windows, but will have indirect light coming in the morning.

I find that eastern-facing windows are a good "catch-all" location and generally good for a large variety of plants. Much of my plant collection grows directly in front of eastern-facing windows. This exposure provides enough light for all plants labeled as low light but also enough light for many

Whenever possible, it is best to situate plants right in front of a window.

plants that need some level of direct sun. We need to keep in mind that the size of the window, and how obstructed or unobstructed the window is outdoors by trees, buildings, and so forth, will affect the light. Not all windows are created equally!

WHY DISTANCE FROM YOUR WINDOWS MATTER

When my followers and readers contact me about their plants that aren't thriving or growing much, I always ask the following simple question: "How far is your plant from a window?"

Although there are many more factors involved in plant care, this is a *critical first question to ask yourself.* Indoors, there isn't nearly as much light as we may think. On top of this, as you get farther and farther from a window, light intensity rapidly declines.

Here is a simple case study that I conducted with a light meter in order to quantify

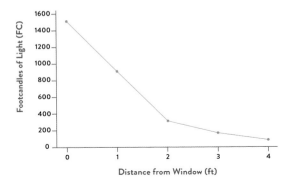

3 feet from the window, it measured 180 FC, or about an 88 percent reduction from the initial reading. At 4 feet, it measured 100 FC, or a 93 percent reduction.

Does this make you rethink the placement of your plants? As you can see, the biggest drop in light intensity happened within the first couple of feet away from the window. As distance increases, light levels continue to drop, but the curve flattens a bit and isn't quite as steep. If you have a really large wall of windows, your profile may look a bit different and light may not decay as dramatically.

What is the moral of the story? Distance from a window matters, and light drops very dramatically the farther you are from a window.

A good rule of thumb, *especially if you are a beginner with houseplants*, is to try and keep your plants within 1 to 2 feet of your windows, or as close as you can get without your plants touching the windows. Depending on what plants you are growing, you would need to consider which window exposure would be best. Of course, there are a handful of houseplants that will still do okay in darker areas. I'll get to that a bit later.

Let's go a bit deeper into the topic of light.

LIGHT INTENSITY INDOORS VERSUS OUTDOORS CASE STUDY

We've just seen how light intensity drops dramatically the farther we get from our windows. Now let's explore another topic

exactly how dramatically light will decrease the farther you move away from a window.

I conducted this simple experiment in front of a south-facing window on a sunny day. I measured the foot-candles (FC) of light at different distances from the window. One FC is simply a measurement of light intensity that is defined as illuminating a one-square-foot area with one lumen of light. FC is a non-SI system measurement. Most of the world uses the SI (International System of Units, which is what we know as the metric system), and in that case, lux would be the SI measurement. In this example, it doesn't matter which measurement I use (FC or lux) because I'm looking at the percent decrease, which will be the same in both cases.

The light reading at one point that almost touched the window was 1500 FC. Moving away from the window just 1 foot resulted in a reading of 900 FC, which is a reduction of 40 percent! At 2 feet from the window, it measured 330 FC, which is about a 78 percent reduction from the initial reading. At

Pothos and peace lily are two plants that can tolerate being far away from a window.

that is important to understand: light intensity.

Light intensity indoors is very different from light intensity outdoors, even if we are literally comparing the same spot on either side of a window. This becomes a very important concept to understand in order to reinforce that we aren't receiving nearly as much light indoors as we think we are.

Here is another simple case study to help you understand this concept. I used my light meter again to measure the foot-candles (FC) of light at the same spot on either side of a sliding glass door in our house that faces approximately southeast.

Indoors, it measured 150 FC. Then I walked outside and held the light meter at the exact same spot, but on the opposite side of the glass. The light meter read 340 FC.

In other words, the light decreased by 56 percent just by passing through the window. The light intensity will continue to decrease indoors as you get farther and farther from the window, as illustrated in the previous section.

Why did the light decrease by more than half as it passed through the glass from outdoors to indoors? The answer might bring back memories of the physics classes you took in school: as light from outside strikes the window, much of the light is reflected and refracted. As a result, the amount of light that comes indoors is reduced. The amount of reduction can vary considerably depending on if the windows are single-paned, double-paned, have certain coatings, contain any insulating gases,

A begonia enjoying a shaded spot outdoors.

and other factors. The bottom line is this: there isn't as much light as you think there is coming through your windows! Not to mention that, more often than not, natural light indoors is typically coming from one direction only (through your window), versus from all directions.

Why does this matter? Because placement of your plant in appropriate light should be the number one decision that you make. Without enough light, your whole journey in houseplant care will be more frustrating, so take this consideration seriously.

I've found that it is pretty difficult indoors to "overdo" light. Your concern should be more about *not enough* versus *too much*. Have you ever burned a houseplant from too much sun? Although it is certainly possible, in many cases it is due to another issue.

I can't tell you how many times my blog readers and followers on Instagram have come to me with burned plants. Everything from rubber plants to string of pearls. The plant parents in question thought they were doing something good for their plants by moving them from indoors to outdoors (in full, direct sun) for a day or two. What started with wonderful intent ended with an unfortunate roasting of their houseplants.

The problem with this scenario is not that rubber plants and string of pearls can't take full sun. Contrary to what many think, they do really well in these conditions! However, you have to be careful about *how abruptly you increase light*. If you abruptly increase the light levels, in this case by putting them outdoors in full sun, your plant will burn, often in a matter of hours! The problem is much worse if your plants were previously growing in very low light conditions indoors.

Moral of the story? Anytime you are increasing light levels for your plants, do so *gradually*. If you are placing any plants outside during warmer weather, be sure to place them in complete shade for several days, and only then add any direct sun very gradually (if your particular plant likes direct sun) to avoid burning. This process is part of what is called hardening off. Likewise, if you have received a plant in the mail that spent some time in a dark box, be sure to gradually increase the light, even indoors.

Think about it this way. I have a pale complexion and my skin is often pasty white, especially during the wintertime. (The winters where I live can be quite dark and depressing!) What would happen if I were to suddenly go to a beach without a base tan and without sunscreen? I will sunburn, and often remarkably fast. The same thing will happen with your plants. Anytime you want to move a plant into much brighter light, you'll have to acclimate your plants slowly by gradually increasing the light so that you're not burning them. Think of it as developing your plant's "base tan."

In most cases that I've seen, the burning of houseplants occurs mostly from not having an acclimation period to higher light. In one case during a consultation with a client, he told me that he had purchased a weeping fig (*Ficus benjamina*) from a store and he immediately placed it in his southern-facing window. Some of the leaves promptly burned, but all the subsequent new growth was fine. Ficus can take plenty of sun, and this was another case of moving a plant from dim lighting in a store (who knows how long the plant was sitting there) to a bright sunny window. This same client was actually keeping a prayer plant in his sunny window with no problems. Yes, a prayer plant, which is a forest floor dweller in the rainforest! This may seem shocking to you, but the lesson is this: unless you live near the equator or in very high altitudes, it is time to reconsider indoor light.

Rubber plants are often labeled as needing low light, but these plants need plenty of bright light, and even direct sun indoors, to really thrive.

I'm not exactly recommending that prayer plants be placed in your sunniest window, but I do encourage you to ditch the conventional information that is rampant and use your personal observations, both physical and visual, to help you.

Many people are scared to give their plants any sliver of direct sun indoors because of the "bright indirect" label they find on their plants. Bright indirect light labels are not instructions to place your plants in a corner far from a window.

Especially if you are a beginner with plants, I encourage you to always place your plants in front of a window. Once you get comfortable with this practice, you can start to break the "rules" and experiment with different placements. There are some plants that will do well pretty far from a window, but until you've become comfortable with growing plants in abundant light, hold off on other placements for now.

HOW CAN YOU TELL IF YOUR PLANT ISN'T GETTING ENOUGH LIGHT?

There are various things that may indicate that your particular plant isn't getting enough light. One big factor is that you simply won't see much growth, and the growth that you do see could result in much smaller leaves than normal. Or if you have a flowering plant, your plant may refuse to flower.

Another telltale sign of not enough light is that your plant will stretch out or etiolate. In many plants, this means that any new growth will be longer and weaker,

and leaves may become spaced out farther from each other than they used to. This is especially apparent in succulents when grown indoors and they don't have enough light. It is tricky with succulents, though, because they typically grow slowly and so the effect of lower light will take a long time to manifest.

Ways to Increase Light for Plants in the Home

- Move them closer to a window.
- Change the window exposure.
- Add mirrors.
- Add full spectrum grow lights.

HOW CAN YOU TELL IF YOUR PLANT IS GETTING TOO MUCH LIGHT?

Sunburn in plants can happen very quickly, especially in cases where you move your plants from indoors to outdoors and don't acclimate them in shade first and then gradually increase light as needed. It can also happen if you bring home a plant that has been sitting at a big-box hardware store indoors in dim lighting and you suddenly place it in a very sunny window without acclimating it first, *even if it's a sun-loving succulent.*

You'll often see large areas of white, or bleached out areas, on the top of the leaves, *and it will happen quickly.* It will be most apparent on the leaves that are most exposed to the sun.

Unfortunately, once sunburn happens

on plants, those leaves will not turn green again, so you may choose to manage your plant by pruning.

If you are blessed with very sunny windows, you can always decrease or diffuse the direct sun with the following methods. It is a good problem to have!

Ways to Decrease Light

- Blinds
- Sheer curtains
- Move your plant a little farther back from your window.

THE MYTH OF LOW-LIGHT PLANTS

Many plants are labeled as low light, and too often people take this to mean that the plants *need* low light. This couldn't be further from the truth. It simply means that the plants will *tolerate* low light. In fact, many of these plants labeled as low light will benefit from at least some direct sun indoors.

At a minimum, even "low-light" plants do best directly in front of a window. Northern-exposure windows (in the Northern Hemisphere) and southern-exposure windows (in the Southern Hemisphere) don't provide any direct sun and "low-light" plants will generally do well in those locations. Many plants, such as pothos, heart leaf philodendron, ZZ plant, snake plants, lucky bamboo, Chinese evergreen, and parlor palm will even survive for a while in nothing but overhead fluorescent lights. I've had offices in the past with no windows and just overhead lighting, and these plants grew and survived for a long time. *But they will do better in brighter light.*

There are some plants that are often listed as low light but are very versatile in the home and actually can even take as much direct sun as you can give them indoors. These include the rubber plant (*Ficus elastica*) and sansevieria (recently reclassified into the *Dracaena* genus). These thrive in anything from your lowest light window to the sunniest window that you have. In my numerous travels around the world, I've seen these plants growing outdoors in very sunny, exposed areas. I've even seen pothos, both as ground covers and rambling up palm trees, in sunny locations in Mexico. *Plants are more versatile than you'd think when it comes to light, especially indoors.*

Remember that light is paramount to the growth of plants, and they use light, in combination with water and carbon dioxide, to photosynthesize and make food for themselves. Deprive them of light, and you deprive them of life. I encourage you to push the limit of your indoor light until you find a suitably bright location for your houseplants. *No photosynthesizing plant can grow in the dark.*

For more specific notes on light for individual plant types, refer to the selection of plants I've included in Plant Party, page 118.

Finally, as mentioned in the Introduction, be wary of plant photos in social media. Often these photos are "styled" and staged, and the plants are not necessarily shown in their growing location! In addition, the

The "cylindrical" snake plant

owners may not have had these plants for long, which can be very misleading. Don't assume that the plants have grown in those specific locations. I've had people tell me that they just want their plants to look like the ones they see on Instagram. Take it for what it's worth: you don't know how long the person has had the plant or if it is even growing in the location shown in the photo. Do not use a social media photo as a decla-ration of its growing conditions. Doing so can lead to many very false assumptions and frustrations. Admire the photos and take them at face value.

Although light is the most important aspect in houseplant care, there are numer-ous other important factors in houseplant care, and it is important to look at plant care *holistically* and not in terms of individual checklist items.

What Is the Humidity Like in My Environment?

A large portion of the plants that we grow as houseplants come from tropical or subtropical, humid climates, and they would appreciate additional humidity in the home.

Unless your plant collection consists of only desert cacti and succulents, it is beneficial to consider increasing your indoor humidity. Many of the plants that we love to grow indoors, such as monsteras, philodendrons, orchids, anthuriums, air plants, prayer plants, ferns, and more, all enjoy higher humidity in their native climates.

In the tropical climates where these plants come from, the relative humidity is commonly in the 70–90 percent range. In the home, this is difficult to achieve and not necessarily practical or necessary. Most houseplants are quite resilient and would be happy in the 40–60 percent relative humidity range. For plants that are native to humid areas, it is always a good practice to increase humidity. This will make the majority of your collection (and your skin) quite happy!

One major benefit of increasing humidity is that it can have a positive effect on soil moisture, especially in the winter. Sometimes in the winter I find that my plants dry out much faster than I would expect. If your humidity is very low, your plants are going to transpire water a lot more rapidly, and this will cause your soil to dry out more quickly. Increasing humidity will help slow this down.

So, how can you measure relative humidity in your home? Invest in a hygrometer. I use one that displays both the relative humidity as well as the temperature.

How do you know if your plants are suffering because of low humidity? Curling leaves, brown leaf tips, and brown leaf edges can all be *potential* indications of low humidity. However, this can be a little tricky to diagnose, given that

Although ferns appreciate high humidity, consistently moist potting mix is much more important.

these can also be signs that your potting mix has been kept too dry. Nature is our best teacher, so you can't go wrong if you attempt to mimic your plant's natural environment. Whenever you increase humidity, don't forget to also increase your air circulation at the same time; this will help discourage any potential fungal issues. A gently circulating fan will do the trick, especially if you have an area with many plants grouped together.

Finally, in my experience, it is far more important to focus on achieving sound watering practices first before blaming low humidity for your plant woes. In many cases, dry soil and improper watering techniques will cause plenty more dry leaves and crispy brown edges on your plants than low humidity ever will.

THE MYTH OF MISTING

Misting houseplants is a widespread practice, but it simply is *not* an effective way to increase humidity. You are essentially just wetting your leaves and not adding any significant amount of moisture to your air. If you overdo misting, constantly wet leaves can also invite fungal issues, not to mention carpal tunnel syndrome in your hands!

I've found two reasons to use my mister that are *not* related to humidity. One is to help deter spider mites. If you have any plants that are prone to spider mites, occasional misting can help deter them. This is because spider mites thrive in warm and dry conditions, so misting can create an unfavorable environment for

them. I mist my aspidistra in the wintertime because it is prone to spider mites, and this has helped manage the issue quite well.

I also like to mist my epiphytic houseplants, such as orchids (particularly exposed roots), bromeliads, *Dischidia,* and others. Epiphytes have evolved to accept moisture through their leaves.

How can you increase humidity?

THREE EFFECTIVE WAYS TO ACTUALLY INCREASE HUMIDITY

Humidifier

The easiest way to increase humidity is to simply use a humidifier. Indoor air can get painfully dry, especially if you live in cold winter regions and use forced air heat to heat your home.

When you purchase a humidifier, pay close attention to the size of the space it is rated for. Good humidifiers will tell you the maximum size of your room it will be effective for.

Also pay special attention to the manufacturer's instructions on how to clean the humidifier. This will help both your humidifier and air stay clean and free of any mold. Some humidifiers have built-in hygrometers to tell you the relative humidity. If yours doesn't, I'd recommend purchasing a separate hygrometer so that you can aim to keep your relative humidity between 40 and 60 percent, which is great for the majority of houseplants. I

Using a humidifier is the most effective way to increase your indoor air humidity.

personally try and keep the humidity in my sunroom, where the majority of my plants are, in the 50–60 percent relative humidity range.

Group Plants Together

Did you know that the simple act of grouping together numerous houseplants will increase humidity? Plants naturally release moisture via their leaves through a process called transpiration. If you group together a lot of plants, you'll be essentially creating a microclimate within your home.

I know this for a fact because my sunroom, which is jam-packed with plants, is often at least 10 percent higher in humidity than the rest of the house, even when I'm not running a humidifier. This is one benefit of being a plant hoarder! Come wintertime though, I do run a humidifier because humidity plummets with our forced air heat.

An *Episcia* sitting on moist pebbles for humidity.

Set Plants on Moist Pebbles

This method is only practical if you have smaller plants and don't have a large collection. Simply make a tray with pebbles, add water so that the water level is just under the pebbles, and then place your houseplants on top. As water evaporates, it will create a more humid microclimate for your plants.

LEFT: Grouping many plants together, like here in my sunroom, can help to increase humidity a bit. But be sure to also provide some air circulation to minimize potential fungal issues.

Key 3.

Where Should I Purchase My Plants?

Whether you are purchasing your houseplants in person at a shop or buying online and having them shipped, I want to discuss what to do with your houseplants once they enter your home, and what you can expect in the first few weeks or months of owning your new plants. The initial transition period is very important, and there are a number of things to be aware of.

BUYING PLANTS: LOCAL NURSERIES AND GREENHOUSES

There are many things to look for when you're selecting a houseplant at a nursery. The first thing I look for is if the nursery looks like it has been lovingly caring for their plants. Is the nursery dirty? Do the plants look neglected? Are there many yellow leaves? Maybe the plants are wilting too? If you've observed any of these things, you may want to look elsewhere. Stressed plants will be more prone to diseases and pests.

It is also important to check your plants for any pests. Look very carefully at the leaves, stems, flowers, and even the surface of the potting mix. Do a thorough visual inspection, including the undersides of leaves, as well as leaf axils where the leaf meets the stem. Pests will often hide in these locations. Do you see anything unusual? Are there maybe spider mite webs, scale, cottony mealy bugs, or fungus gnats flying around? If so, you may want to visit another nursery and not bring home a pest-infested plant.

The next suggestion may seem odd, but go ahead and smell the surface of your pot-

Mail ordering plants is a convenient way to increase your collection, but there are many things to consider when purchasing plants online.

ting mix. Does it small rancid or foul? If so, the plant in question probably has root rot and you should avoid purchasing it. If you've observed a foul odor, you'll probably also notice that the growing medium is soggy and the plant is perhaps sitting in water.

Is the foliage free of any spots? Spots can be an indication of bacterial or fungal diseases, so avoid bringing these plants back home.

Finally, if you are able to look at the roots, go ahead and do so with permission. In many cases, you can easily slip a root-bound plant out of its pot. It is easiest to do if the plant is growing in a flexible nursery pot and the pot

is small. This is by no means a requirement, but it can be helpful sometimes. Root color can vary, but healthy roots will always be firm. If you observe any squishy roots and the root system doesn't appear particularly vigorous, avoid that plant. If it's not practical to remove a plant from the pot, you may be able to take a peek through the drainage holes and inspect the roots. Some plants, like many orchids, are sometimes grown in clear plastic pots, in which case it is easy to inspect the roots without disturbing the plant.

Choosing the healthiest, most vigorous plant that you can will help you avoid many frustrations down the line.

For many of us, local nurseries have a limited supply of plants. As a result, the mail ordering of plants has exploded in popularity. There are quite a few things to be aware of when purchasing plants online.

Buying Plants Online: What to Be Aware Of

The benefits to buying plants online are many, but there are also many things to keep in mind so that you have the best experience possible. Nothing beats having a staggering selection of plants right at your fingertips.

Whether you're buying from an established, well-known nursery; from eBay, Etsy, or Facebook groups; or from individual sellers, here is what you should know:

- Pay special attention to the description in the online listing and read the whole description. Are the photos of the actual plant that you will receive? Although you may assume they are, this is often not the case! A good seller will indicate something like "photo shows the exact plant that is up for sale." If the description doesn't say that, there should be at least a good description of the plant itself, such as pot size, plant size, number of leaves, and other details. Sometimes a photo of a potted plant will be shown, but the seller is actually selling a cutting. Read everything carefully to avoid disappointment! If you have questions, contact the seller and ask. You can even request photos

of the actual plants that would be shipped if those weren't provided.

- If you're buying a cutting, make sure the seller indicates if it is rooted or not. Don't make any assumptions.
- Be wary of common names of plants in online listings that show several descriptions or names. You may want to avoid these sellers. Often, there are multiple common names for plants, and it can be very confusing. Once I purchased a cutting of what was supposed to be *Dischidia nummularia.* The photo showed a potted *Dischidia nummularia,* and the listing contained all the following names: *Dischidia nummularia,* button orchid, ant plant, and string of nickels. When I received the shipment, not only was it just a cutting and not a potted plant, but it was the wrong plant! The cutting was not a *Dischidia nummularia,* but rather a *Xerosicyos danguyi!* After filing a complaint, I got my money back.
- If you see typos or weird language in online listings, you may want to avoid those sellers.
- Always read the reviews of the seller if they are available. It will give you an idea of how many transactions that seller has completed and how happy the buyers were.
- Shop around! Look at multiple listings and see what the best deal is, but also check the size and weight of the plant and other factors. Don't forget to look at shipping costs as well. Many times, it will be much

more than the plant itself. Sometimes you can add more plants and your shipping costs will stay the same or increase only a small amount. Try and get the most bang for your buck when you can.

- Sometimes the seller will have a pot size listed. Don't be fooled by this. What is more important is the size of the plant itself. Sometimes sellers will ultimately place a very small plant in a pot much too large for it. The pot size will give a false illusion that the plant you will be receiving is much larger than it really is. Along those lines, a description of the plant itself will be much more important than the indicated pot size. The best case would be to see an actual picture of the plant you will be receiving. This would give you everything you need to know.

- Finally, if you are buying plants from another country, a phytosanitary certificate is often necessary. So make sure that your international seller is able to ship to your country and has a phytosanitary certificate for the sale. This certificate states that the plants being shipped are free of pests and diseases and also will conform to any other current phytosanitary regulations defined by the importing country. These documents are important in helping to prevent the spread of pests and diseases to other countries, which can cause a lot of harm to local flora.

DOS AND DON'TS WHEN RECEIVING PLANTS IN THE MAIL

I've coached many people on this topic. All too often, plant parents are too eager to do a number of things with their plants, such as repotting and fertilizing, as soon as they receive them. Knowing what to do, and what not to do, with your houseplants after you've unboxed them will start your plants off on the right foot!

Dos

UNPACK YOUR BOX IMMEDIATELY! Your plant has spent a good deal of time sitting in a dark box waiting for its new home. Be very aware of when your shipments are arriving, especially during colder months. Know where the nursery is geographically, and also be mindful of your own weather during the shipping period. It may be best to avoid trying to buy houseplants by mail during very cold weather. Good nurseries will ship with heat packs during cooler weather, and they will even suspend shipping during very cold periods. Many of the houseplants we grow in the home are native to tropical regions and despise cold weather, so this can be a dangerous proposition.

Be sure to track your package. If you won't be home for a while, have someone pick up the box and bring it indoors. Extreme cold or heat will shock your plant.

Carefully unpack all of your plants as soon as you can. Remove any packing

Be sure to immediately unpack your plants when you receive them in the mail.

materials such as plastic, tape, and shredded paper that were used to protect the plant during shipping. If you see any dead or broken leaves, go ahead and remove those.

WATER YOUR PLANT IMMEDIATELY IF IT IS DRY. Check the potting medium of your plant with your finger. Is the surface dry? Go ahead and give it a good watering if it is dry, especially if it is completely dry. If the potting medium still feels damp to the touch, you should hold off.

INCREASE HUMIDITY. This isn't necessary, but it may help your plant make a smoother transition, especially if your plant looks a little less than ideal when it arrives. If you have a small plant, you can simply insert a couple of bamboo sticks into the pot of your new plant. Ensure that the sticks are taller than the plant. Then cover the plant with a clear plastic bag, leaving plenty of room for the plant to breathe. Be sure to keep it out of direct sun, so your plant doesn't cook under the bag. Key 2 (page 32) of this book describes other methods to increase humidity.

Don'ts

DON'T REPOT YOUR PLANT IMMEDI-ATELY. Your plant has just suffered in a dark box in transit to your home, so wait at least a couple weeks before you repot your plant. This will give it time to adjust to its new environment. If your plant is root-bound, wait a couple weeks, and then go up only one pot size from the previous pot. If your plant is not root-bound, there is no need to move it to another pot. Refer to Key 5 (page 64) for more details on this topic.

DON'T START FERTILIZING RIGHT AWAY. Wait at least two weeks in order to allow your plant to adjust or you may be further shocking your plant. You don't want to fertilize a stressed or shocked plant.

DON'T PLACE YOUR PLANT INTO BRIGHT LIGHT RIGHT AWAY. This goes even for plants that need direct sun! Your plant just spent some time in a dark box, so gradually acclimate your plant to brighter light in order to avoid leaf burn. Place your plant in front of a window that doesn't receive any direct sun for at least two weeks. Then at that point, if your specific plant requires direct sun, you can gradu-

Watering my *Peperomia* 'Hope'

ally increase the light until it is in its final growing location.

DON'T WATER IF THE SOIL OR POTTING MEDIUM IS ALREADY MOIST. Resist the urge! So many people rush to automatically repot and water everything immediately, but sometimes it pays to just hold off and let things be. If the surface of your potting medium is moist, then hold off a little longer.

AVOID PLACING YOUR PLANTS IN AREAS WITH COLD OR HOT DRAFTS. This applies for any situation, but especially with new plants.

WHAT TO EXPECT WITH YOUR NEW PLANTS

If you are selecting a plant at a nursery, be sure to inspect it for pests before purchasing. Check the leaves, including the undersides of the leaves, petioles, stems, and flowers for any potential pests. If you're ordering by mail, you're at the mercy of the vendor, but still inspect your plant when you take it out of the box. If you see anything unusual, you may want to quarantine your plant and make any treatment if necessary.

Whether you brought your plant home from a nursery or received it by mail, there are some important things to expect in the first few weeks or months of owning your new houseplant.

First, don't freak out if you get a yellow leaf or two. This is not uncommon. It is important to remember that the plant went from the ideal growing conditions of a greenhouse to the average indoor growing conditions of your home. You may not see yellow leaves on every plant, but don't be shocked if you do. Allow your plant to adjust.

If your plant has unopened flower buds, you may see that some of the buds wither or drop before they open. This is known as bud blast. Bud blast can happen for a variety of reasons, but it is not uncommon for plants that experience a drastic change in environment. It doesn't necessarily mean your plant is dying! It just means your plant needs to adjust to your home environment. Bud blast commonly happens with phalaenopsis orchids as well as Christmas cactus, where the unopened buds may dry up before they even open.

Finally, don't have high expectations for growth right away. Some houseplants are more robust than others, but if you don't see growth right away, it is okay! Try and have a little patience, do your best to supply your plant with the necessary care, and trust that it will start growing after it becomes adjusted to your home. However, it is ultimately up to you to provide the correct conditions.

RIGHT: Prayer plant (*Maranta leuconeura*)

PART TWO

What Does Routine Care Look Like for My Plants?

So you've evaluated your habitat, and you've ensured that your plants have enough light and humidity to thrive.

Now that you've done this and found your perfect plant, you can freely focus, without worry, on the routine aspects of houseplant care. These tasks include proper techniques for watering, fertilizing, and everything related to repotting or up-potting your plants. This section discusses these aspects of houseplant care in detail.

It's important to keep in mind that part of the routine care of your houseplants includes maintaining clean and hygienic conditions for your plants. Remove any fully yellowed or brown leaves that may develop on your plants. This is not just simply for good appearance, it also helps to discourage conditions that may attract various pests. Although yellowing leaves are not necessarily a cause for alarm, it's a matter that should be addressed. See Part 3 for help diagnosing *why* they are occurring.

Finally, don't forget to keep your plants clean! I like to take plants periodically to the sink or shower and rinse them off with tepid water (except for ones with hairy leaves). Washing off any accumulated dust and keeping the leaves clean will go a long way toward keeping a plant healthy. If your plants are too big to move easily, use a moist sponge or paper towel to gently wipe off any dust.

In order to discourage any potential for rotting, as well as fungal diseases, ensure that your plant can dry out in a reasonable time. If you are rinsing off your plants, be sure to remove any water that happens to be stuck in the crown of your plant (or in any other nooks and crannies), and then ensure that the leaves dry out quickly. I like to accomplish this

Dead leaves removed from my *Pilea peperomioides*.

by gently circulating the air with the ceiling fan in my sunroom. Air circulation is often ignored as a topic in plant care, but gently circulating air can go a long way toward preventing fungal issues, especially if you have a lot of houseplants crammed in together.

LEFT: Several dried-up leaves removed from the base of my ponytail palm (*Beaucarnea recurvata*).

Key 4.

How Should I Water and Fertilize?

Proper watering is an absolutely crucial aspect of houseplant care. It is essential to understand this, because it will make the difference between a thriving houseplant and one that languishes.

Throughout all my experience helping people every day with plant problems, I've seen the repercussions of incorrect watering and fertilization practices. In this chapter, I'll go over exactly how and when to water and fertilize a houseplant, and why these methods are important.

HOW TO WATER A HOUSEPLANT

First, let me describe how to properly water your houseplant, regardless of what kind of houseplant you have. I'll then go through many common watering practices and pitfalls that can lead to poor plant growth.

The procedure is really as simple as following these steps:

- Use room temperature water or even warm water (never cold). Remember that most houseplants come from warm regions of the world, so it makes sense to avoid cold water.
- Circle your watering can around the entire surface of the pot.
- Keep adding water until water starts to escape the drainage hole. The goal is to thoroughly moisten *all* of the soil.
- If there is excess water in the saucer under your pot, discard the excess water and don't allow the pot to sit in standing water. If you have your plant growing in a pot with drainage holes, and it is slipped into a cachepot (a decorative pot with no drainage holes), also be sure to discard any excess water. Failing to do so can result in root rot, so always check!

Learning how to water and fertilize properly are musts for healthy plant growth.

Watering my Chinese evergreen plant in the bathtub to make discarding excess water easy.

My favorite way to water, and it works really well for smaller plants, is to take my plants to the kitchen or bathroom sink or shower and water them there. It is a bit more work, but it ensures a *thorough* moistening of the soil and it makes much less of a mess. You can also easily give them a gentle shower this way to wash off the leaves.

Do I always take my smaller pots to the sink at every watering? No. But I try to do it as many times as possible when my plants need watering.

For larger plants that are too big and heavy to move, I obviously water those in place. You still should water until water escapes the drainage holes. Don't be tempted to leave the pot sitting in water. If excess water has accumulated in the saucer, you can use a turkey baster to suck out all the excess water.

Once, I got lazy and let my Norfolk Island pine sit in water that had accumulated in the saucer. I knew better, but I'm human and sometimes laziness sets in! The soil stayed wet for weeks and the whole plant started to droop. Before any permanent damage could be done, I took out my turkey baster, removed the excess water, and waited. Slowly the plant went back to normal. If I had waited even a little while longer, it would have suffered irreparable harm and root rot.

MYTH OF OVERWATERING

The term *overwatering* is very widespread and has caused a lot confusion for too many people. For some reason, whenever a plant is suffering, many people immediately think that they have a case of overwatering. I'm including a section on this topic because I've heard it ad nauseam and it merits a healthy discussion.

Often, the verdict of overwatering will be given without even *observing* the soil moisture. Readers frequently write in to ask for help with yellowing leaves, assuming that they are the result of overwatering. (For an example of this, see Case #3 in Case Studies, page 96.) In most cases, after we chat about soil moisture, the plant parent discovers that the soil is actually dry. For this reason, I always suggest that you check soil moisture with your fingers.

I can't tell you how many times I've had this conversation. In the case of yellow leaves, there are several things that can cause them, so you must *observe your conditions* and determine why it occurred. Make no mistake, observation is truly a game changer: you must make physical observations about your plants and not trust certain statements blindly.

Sometimes, people are too scared to water properly. Because of the fear of overwatering, they will measure out set amounts of water and not even moisten all of the plant's soil. I've had many people tell me that they measure out 2 or 3 tablespoons of water for their succulents because they're afraid of overwatering. This amount of water will not suffice, and the plant will suffer over time because its root system will suffer with this kind of watering. The roots that don't get any water will eventually desiccate and die. Without a healthy root system, your plant will languish and you will see all sorts of issues. It is not necessary to measure out the water. Your goal should be to thoroughly moisten your soil.

Another one of my readers sent me photos of his dragon tree (*Dracaena marginata*). The entire plant was drooping and an excessive number of lower leaves had turned brown. I was able to get down to the bottom of the issue with a simple question, "How do you water?"

He mentioned that he added half a pint of water to what looked like a 10-inch pot or so. Half a pint will not suffice for that size pot. He needed to provide the plant with more water. Problem solved.

As a general rule of thumb, *the way in which you water any plant, regardless of the type, is the same.* You must thoroughly moisten the potting mix. *All* of the potting mix. Even for succulents! *Whether you are watering a fern or a cactus, the way you should water is the same.*

What you *do* need to vary is how dry you allow the soil to become before you water again. Ferns like to stay pretty consistently moist to be happy, whereas cacti need to dry out completely and can stay dry for extended periods. Most indoor houseplants like something in between. For suggestions regarding soil moisture levels for specific plants, see Plant Party, page 118.

The reason I despise the term *over-*

watering is because it drives the wrong behavior. The term *overwatering* makes it seem like it is related to the amount of water that you actually add to your plant. The danger in overwatering has nothing to do with the amount of water that you add to your plants, but rather *how wet your soil stays over time.*

If I may be so bold, I would like to ask that you never say the word *overwatering* again. This word might be engrained into your vocabulary, and it could be difficult to break free from it. The first step is to know that there is no such thing as overwatering.

With this in mind, instead of saying "I overwatered my plant," or "I underwatered my plant," try some statements that are more helpful:

- My potting mix is too wet.
- My potting mix is too dry.

But in order to make such statements, you need to *make an observation* and not automatically assume that your plant is suffering because you overwatered. By observation, what I mean is that you should use your finger and actually *feel the potting mix.* This is something that I cannot emphasize enough.

If you have watered the way I describe, and you have issues with your potting mix staying too wet (or worse yet, your plant has root rot), there are bigger issues that you should consider correcting. These corrections include increasing your light, having an appropriately sized pot (with a drainage hole), and using a well-draining potting mix. I'll discuss how these factors all work together later on.

Finally, I should perhaps mention one case where it is possible to overwater. Namely, if you use pots without drainage holes. I don't recommend this practice, but I discuss this more a bit later. Please see Pot Types on page 69.

JUDGING SOIL MOISTURE

Some people swear by moisture meters and use them to gauge soil moisture to help them determine if they should water their plants. If you are happy with your particular meter and are happy with the health and appearance of your houseplants, I'm by no means going to tell you to change. Like the saying goes: if it ain't broke, don't fix it!

That said, I've worked with many clients who killed their plants because they relied on moisture meters. For example, one friend of mine reached out for help with her houseplants and told me the following: "Do you have any suggestions as to how to keep these plants from dying? I use a water meter and I haven't needed to water them for months."

After *months* of not watering, the moisture meter still read MOIST. As a result, her rubber plant suffered defoliation. One stem lost all of its leaves. Other stems still had leaves, but they were contorted and dry.

The inexpensive moisture meters that are often sold in hardware stores are often junky, give false readings, and do much more damage than good. In fact, moisture meters don't even read the moisture level. They actually attempt to measure conductivity. While water is a good conductor of electricity, the readings from these meters may not accurately reflect soil moisture. And depending on the composition of your potting mix, you can see wildly different and misleading results.

Instead of a moisture meter, here are some better ways to judge soil moisture levels:

- Your finger is your best friend to help you judge soil moisture. This is what I rely on and, over time, you will learn to rely on it more and more.
- Another option is to insert a plain bamboo chopstick into the soil at least a couple of inches deep. Take the chopstick out after 10–15 minutes and evaluate the color. If the part of the chopstick that was in the soil has darkened, it's an indication that it has absorbed water. This means you can likely wait to water in most cases, especially for plants that like to dry out completely, like many succulents, cacti, hoyas, and others. If there is no color change at all, you'll probably want to water regardless of what type of plant you have.
- Picking up your plant and judging the weight can be a great indication of soil moisture. After you water your plant, pick up the pot and see how heavy it feels. Then lift your plant every few days. When the soil is very dry, your plant will feel much lighter.

You'll need to get to know the moisture needs of each individual plant to determine how dry you should allow your potting mix to become. This determination will come with time, experimentation, and

Using the finger test to judge potting mix moisture levels.

experience. I have included general guidelines in the plant profiles at the end of this book to assist you. Please see Plant Party on page 118.

WHY WATERING SCHEDULES ARE TRICKY

One of the most common questions posed to me by my readers and followers is, "How often should I water my [insert type of plant here]?"

Many people are stuck on the "once a

week" watering routine. A schedule is a great thing to have as a checkpoint, but be careful of using a strict schedule to definitively tell you when you should be watering your plants. Granted, in some cases, once a week will work fine temporarily. But strict watering schedules like this are not ideal in the long term because many environmental factors affect how quickly or slowly your soil is drying out. My indoor conditions are not the same as your indoor conditions. So how can I possibly tell you how often to water your plant?

Even if you adhere to a consistent watering schedule, many things *are* constantly changing throughout the year that end up affecting how quickly your potting mix is drying out. Your once-a-week schedule may indeed work for a while, but there will come a time when it will fail you.

As a plant parent, you need to be aware of various factors that affect how quickly your potting mix dries out:

- **LIGHT.** As you increase light for your houseplants, they will grow more and end up using more water, thus your potting mix will dry out more quickly. If you have plants growing in very dim conditions, you may find that your potting mix takes a long time to dry out. In addition, natural light can change dramatically throughout the seasons, which in turn affects soil moisture levels.
- **TYPE AND SIZE OF POTS.** Pots make a *huge* difference in how fast soil dries. Soil in small pots dries out much more quickly than soil in larger ones. Terra cotta pots also dry out soil much more quickly than

plastic pots or even glazed pots. This is because terra cotta pots are extremely porous and don't block the flow of air. I've struggled with tiny terra cotta pots for this reason. If you use them, be sure to check up on your plants regularly!

- **HANGING PLANTS.** Plants placed in higher locations tend to dry out faster than plants located near the floor. Remember that heat rises, so the air around your hanging plants is likely warmer than the air around the plants lower down near the floor. On the same note, potting mixes dry out much more quickly in warmer rooms versus cooler rooms.
- **HUMIDITY.** Plants that are in warm rooms with low humidity (which is typical if you use forced air heat in your home) will dry out more quickly. Increasing the humidity in your air will help slow down the rate at which your soil dries out. Drier air (lower humidity) will increase the rate of transpiration in your plant, and your soil will dry out more quickly. Through the process of transpiration, plants release water vapor through openings in leaves called stomata. If you increase humidity, the transpiration rate will decrease and your potting mix won't dry out as quickly.
- **THE POTTING MIX COMPOSITION.** The composition of the soil affects how quickly it dries out. Mixes that contain a higher percentage of water-absorbent materials like peat moss

Terra cotta pots are great for plants that need to dry out quickly, such as snake plants. Avoid terra cotta for moisture-loving plants.

will retain water much more than other mixes. On the other hand, many commercially available cactus and succulent mixes use sand, which helps to increase drainage but absorbs very little water.

- **TEMPERATURE.** Up to a certain point, many plant processes such as photosynthesis and transpiration increase as the temperature increases and thus affect soil moisture.

Why does all this matter? It matters because knowledge is power. Many people have reached out to me with the following plea: *"I don't understand why my plant isn't doing well anymore. I haven't changed a thing! I was watering once a week for a long time and then my plant started to suffer and I don't know why!"*

If you follow a strict watering schedule, just know it may work temporarily but it will not work forever. Even though *you* may not change anything, your plant *will* grow and change; and on top of that, environmental conditions are constantly changing throughout the year. It is important to be a flexible plant parent and water when it is *needed* versus when your calendar tells you to do it.

WHAT TO DO WHEN YOUR SOIL HAS GONE BONE DRY

Sometimes when potting mix becomes really dry, so dry that it pulls away from the edges of the pot, we have to put some work in to get it back to "normal." This is a very common problem that many people don't even realize they have. Have you ever let a plant dry out so much that when you went to water it, the water seemed to just stream straight through and barely any was actually absorbed into the potting mix?

Why does this happen? Your potting mix probably became hydrophobic, which means that it repels water. Some potting mixes, particularly ones that contain peat moss, become very hydrophobic when they dry out and are very difficult to rewet.

To ensure that you can rehydrate your potting soil so that it accepts water once again, here are some techniques you can use:

- Bottom water your plant and let it soak up water over time. Simply place your pot in a container of shallow water and let it sit there for at least an hour or more. Use tepid or warm water, keep monitoring the water level, and replenish as needed. Once you can feel moisture on the surface of the soil, or close to it, you should be all set. Lift your pot out and allow excess water to drain away completely. Your pot should feel much heavier than it did when you started.
- You can also take a bucket of water and submerge the whole pot. Hold the pot down with your hands. You will see a lot of air bubbles coming up as the water displaces the air. Leave the pot submerged for a few minutes, lift the pot out, and let it fully drain.

Hanging plants, like this *Philodendron hederaceum* 'Brasil,' can dry out more quickly than plants near the floor.

A bottom-watering system I set up for a few of my succulents.

- One last option is to slowly trickle water into the pot. This is a good technique if your pot is too big to bottom water or if you can't find a container big enough for the submersion technique. If it is raining outside and temperatures are adequate for your plant, place it outside and let Mother Nature do the work for you. You can also trickle water very slowly from a hose or faucet.

BOTTOM WATERING VERSUS TOP WATERING

Although I personally am a top-watering plant parent, there are a couple of cases where bottom watering can be useful.

There is really no need to elaborate much on top watering. This is simply how most of us are used to watering our plants. We add water with a watering can over the top of the potting mix and allow it to soak in, with excess water escaping the pot's drainage hole. Top watering is definitely much easier, quicker, and less risky compared to bottom watering.

Although no plant really *needs* to be bottom watered, I have found it to come in handy in a couple cases. One case is when your potting mix has gone bone dry.

Another case in which you would use bottom watering is if a plant has a crown that is so dense and thick that there is no room to insert the nozzle of a watering can to properly water the soil. I have an echeveria that fits this description. The plant is growing in a plastic pot with drainage holes and it is slipped into a cachepot. I simply lift out the plastic pot, fill the cachepot with water, place the plant in, and let it soak up the water for a while, even for a few hours. Then I lift the plant out of the cachepot, discard the excess water, and return the plant to the cachepot. If you do this, don't forget to discard the excess water, otherwise your plant may rot! I have forgotten on a handful of occasions and left it soaking in water for a day, but fortunately the plant was still okay.

These are the only two cases that I would use bottom watering. Some people swear by bottom watering African violets. Others claim that bottom watering helps control fungus gnats because it keeps the top portion of soil in the pot drier, and this makes it less likely that the eggs and/or larvae will survive. Fungus gnats need moist soil to proliferate. I've never had any issues top watering any African violets, probably because I do let them dry out appropriately. I have never used bottom watering to manage fungus gnats, but if it works for you, keep doing it!

Be aware that bottom watering can cause an accumulation of fertilizer salts

This *Pilea peperomioides* has dried out so much that the potting mix has pulled away from the edge of the pot.

and also minerals from tap water. If you regularly bottom water your plants, make sure to top water with plain water periodically in order to flush out any accumulated salts or minerals that can damage your plant. Simply top water with plain water until it flushes out of the drainage hole.

WHY IT IS IMPORTANT TO FERTILIZE

In nature, plants have the benefit of receiving nutrients from various sources: decaying leaves and branches, animal droppings, and even rainwater, which contains nitrates, a very bio-available form of nitrogen. Since we don't have these things occurring inside our homes, we need to compensate by using fertilizer.

Fertilizer should by no means be used to make up for cultural shortcomings, such as insufficient light. If you have a sickly plant in a dark area of your home and it is not growing well, your first order of business would be to supply enough light for the plant before even thinking about fertilizing. Any plants in dim locations need very little to no fertilizing simply because they are either growing very little or not at all. In addition, most succulents won't need much fertilizing, though they will benefit from a couple of applications of fertilizer during the growing season.

NPK RATIOS

You'll always see three numbers on any fertilizer label. This is called the NPK ratio. If you've taken chemistry in school, these should look familiar because they represent the chemical symbols for nitrogen (N), phosphorous (P), and potassium (K). These are often referred to as the primary nutrients or macronutrients because plants need large amounts of them.

The fertilizer I use for most of my plants has an NPK ratio of 7-9-5. To put it simply, the numbers refer to the relative percentage of nitrogen, phosphorus, and potassium that the fertilizer contains. There are many formulations out there. They include balanced fertilizers (10-10-10, for example) and many all-purpose formulations of varying NPK ratios. Pick one that you like and make it a part of your houseplant care routine.

I like to keep it simple and use one fertilizer for most of my plants, but I also use more specialized fertilizers to meet the specific needs of certain plants. Fertilizers for succulents and cacti are generally much lower in nitrogen (for example, 2-7-7). There are also "bloom booster" fertilizers that have a higher percentage of phosphorus (for example, 10-30-20). Keep in mind that the most important factor for flowering to occur is light! Bloom booster fertilizers will only enhance your show.

What is the function of these primary nutrients? Nitrogen (N) promotes leafy growth. Phosphorus (P) assists with encouraging both flowering and root growth. Potassium (K) is necessary for many important physiological processes in plants, as well as for disease resistance, cold tolerance, and protection against drought.

Plants also need some secondary nutrients in lesser amounts, as well as important micronutrients in very small amounts. Using a premium fertilizer that contains all of the macro- and micronutrients will safeguard against any nutrient deficiencies and be an important part of any houseplant care regimen.

It is always important to follow the manufacturer's dilution instructions when measuring the fertilizer or the water. If the fertilizer is too diluted, that's not a problem. The problem comes if you're not measuring carefully and your solution is too concentrated with fertilizer. Fertilizer burn is real and can manifest itself in brown leaf margins or even yellowing leaves.

When I fertilize, I use a dedicated set of

measuring spoons to measure the fertilizer, and I use an empty plastic jug to measure the water. In this way, I can be sure that I have the exact solution I intended. Never eyeball or freehand the amount of fertilizer or water!

WHEN TO FERTILIZE

You should only fertilize your houseplants during periods of active growth. My houseplants are actively growing from about late February through October or so. During wintertime, when natural light is greatly reduced, I normally refrain from fertilizing.

Succulents and cacti don't really need much fertilizer. I might fertilize mine two or three times during the growing season.

HOW TO FERTILIZE

The fertilizer that I use specifies ¼ to ½ teaspoon per gallon of water to be used at every watering. This mimics the way that plants receive nutrients in nature, which is slow and steady.

If your fertilizer label tells you to use 1 teaspoon per gallon once a month, I would divide the amount of fertilizer by four and use ¼ teaspoon per gallon at every watering, whenever you need to water. You could go with the more concentrated solution

Measuring my fertilizer to mix with water.

once a month, but I find it safer to use a diluted fertilizer with every watering.

Over time, fertilizer salts can build up in the soil and become toxic to your plants. Periodically, be sure to water with plain water until water streams through the drainage hole in order to flush any excess salts out of your soil.

Remember that less is more when it comes to fertilizing, and you should never use fertilization as a Band-Aid for poor cultural conditions such as insufficient light. It should supplement a plant's health and growth after you have nailed down the appropriate light requirements and have established sound watering practices.

Key 5.

How Can I Make Good Choices about Pots, Repotting, and Potting Mixes?

REPOTTING

If you closely observe your plants, they will give you many signals to indicate if they need repotting. Observing one or more of the following *may* indicate that your plant needs a larger pot:

- You see a lot of roots coming out of the drainage hole(s).
- There is no more soil at the surface of the pot. Instead, you see a hard mat of roots.
- Your plant either stopped growing or it is starting to suffer. However, it's important to note that a lack of growth does not always mean that you need to repot. Analyze other factors first. If you have your plant in a dark corner somewhere, the reason

it's not growing is because it doesn't have enough light!
- You may notice that your soil is drying out much more quickly than it used to, despite frequent watering. This is sometimes the most important indicator that a plant needs to be repotted.

Of course, you won't know exactly how root-bound the plant is until you take it out of its pot.

This ponytail palm (*Beaucarnea recurvata*) is root-bound and is ready for a bigger pot.

Before getting into the steps for repotting, here are some important tips to prepare for repotting your plants:

- **SPRING IS *GENERALLY* THE BEST TIME TO REPOT YOUR PLANTS.** Spring is the time of year when your plants are starting back up into active growth. I repot the bulk of my plants in spring and summer. Is it the only time to repot? No! But until you have some experience under your belt, try not to repot in the wintertime, when plants aren't growing much, unless you have an emergency. If you live in a climate that is bright and sunny year-round and your plants are growing year-round, you can repot whenever you need to. If you live in a less than ideal climate with dark winters, like I do, but permanently grow your plants under grow lights, then go ahead and repot when you need to!

- **IF YOUR SOIL IS REALLY DRY, WATER YOUR PLANT AND WAIT A DAY BEFORE REPOTTING.** This will make it easier to loosen the root ball, handle the roots, and minimize damage.

- **AS A GENERAL RULE, IT IS SAFER TO GO UP ONLY ONE POT SIZE.** For example, if your plant is currently growing in a 4-inch diameter pot, go up to a 6-inch diameter pot. If you go from a 4-inch pot to an 8-inch

Watering one of my plants before repotting to make it easier to loosen the roots.

pot, let's say, there will be a disproportionally large volume of soil and it will take much longer to dry out, which can cause you a headache. For certain plants that need to dry out relatively quickly, this poses an issue and can be a contributing factor to root rot. Down the line you can break this "rule" as you become more comfortable with plant care and develop more of an intuition.

- **ALWAYS USE POTS WITH DRAINAGE HOLES!** Although it is possible to grow plants in pots with no drainage holes, doing so will often lead to problems. Multiple things can go wrong, including adding too much water at one time, which contributes to root rot (given that the water has nowhere to go). No drainage holes can also cause an accumulation of fertilizer salts or a buildup of minerals from tap water, which can eventually harm your plants. Spare yourself all the worry and use pots with drainage holes.

STEPS TO REPOTTING

1. Remove your plant from the pot. If it is still in a plastic nursery pot, gently squeeze the pot around the perimeter, and then slowly pull the plant out. If you have a rigid pot, run a knife around the inside perimeter of the pot in an attempt to loosen the root ball from the pot itself. Tip the pot over, grasp the plant at the base, and gently pull it out. If you have a terra cotta pot or a ceramic pot and you are worried that you won't be able

to safely remove your plant without damaging it, take a hammer to the pot and break it! I've done this many times in cases where the plant is worth much more to me than the pot.

2. Next, you'll want to loosen the root ball a bit. *Don't skip this step.* You don't have to go crazy, but this step is especially important if there are many roots circled around and they are tightly packed. Work to loosen the very bottom of the root ball first, then loosen the roots around the sides. Loosen what you can, remove any loose potting soil, and cut off any roots that are rotten or mushy. If you have a heavily root-bound plant and you don't loosen it, the plant will have a very difficult time growing into the new soil in its new pot.

I can't emphasize enough the part about loosening your root ball. This is absolutely essential, particularly if you have a severely root-bound plant. Many years ago, before I knew any better, I had placed a peace lily that was severely root-bound into a larger pot. It stayed there for quite a while and was languishing slowly, though I wasn't quite sure why. After a couple of years, I decided to remove it from the pot, and I discovered that there wasn't a *single* root that had grown into the new soil! This was because the root ball had not been loosened. In fact, the roots were still as tightly wound as they had been when I initially repotted it! Needless to say, I then loosened the root ball and placed the plant back into the larger pot. The resulting growth was luxurious.

A severely root-bound plant before loosening the root ball.

After loosening the root ball, it is ready for a bigger pot.

3. Cover the drainage hole with either a broken pot shard or a fine mesh screen. This isn't 100 percent necessary, but doing this will keep the soil in while allowing water to drain through. I have plenty of broken terra cotta pots that I've saved for this purpose. Position the pot shard over the hole so that the orientation is like an upside-down U over the drainage hole. Some people are against using pot shards, but they've worked well for me. If you don't have any pot shards, you can use a fine mesh screen (either from old window screens or mesh pads meant for bonsai). Ultimately, use what you're comfortable with. Always use pots with drainage holes. It is too risky not to!

4. Place some potting mix at the bottom of the new pot. It will take a little trial and error to place your plant at the right level. Hold the plant in the center of the pot and continue to add potting mix but *don't add soil all the way up to the top of the pot.* Gently press the soil down a bit to ensure there are no big air pockets. I always leave about half an inch or so from the soil line to the rim of the pot. This will act as a reservoir for watering. Otherwise, if you add soil all the way to the top of the pot, you will wind up making a mess and it will be harder to give the plant a thorough watering.

5. Finally, give your plant a nice thorough watering in a sink and let excess water drain away. You may find that the soil will settle and the soil level will go down. If this is the case, go ahead and add a little more potting mix to make up for it. Then place your plant in its growing location.

POT TYPES

There are many types of pots out there that we can use for our houseplants, and each type has its pros and cons. Here are some of the most common types and the pros and cons I've found from using each one.

Plastic Nursery Pots

There are many pros to using plastic nursery pots. Although they are not that attractive, I often plant many houseplants inside flexible plastic pots and then slip them inside of a cachepot, which is basically a decorative pot. Why would I do this? One of the main advantages of keeping plants in a nursery pot is that *repotting is so much easier*. It is far easier to take a plant out of this type of pot than out of ones that are more rigid. And I can still slip the plant inside a decorative pot for aesthetic purposes if I choose to do so.

Plastic pots are also inexpensive, are more lightweight, and will keep your soil from drying out too quickly, given that they are not porous.

Terra Cotta Pots

Terra cotta literally means "baked earth" in Italian, and as the name suggests, it is essentially baked clay. There are many advantages to terra cotta pots, including price. They are indeed inexpensive. They are also extremely porous and can allow potting mix to dry out terribly quickly! This can be both a good thing and a bad thing. If you have plants that need to dry out relatively quickly in between watering, such as any succulent or cactus, terra cotta pots are a great choice.

If your tendency is to keep your potting mix too moist, terra cotta might be a good choice for you. Because of the porous nature of terra cotta and the fact that they allow potting mix to dry out pretty quickly, it would be counterproductive to plant

TOP: Two succulents in plastic nursery pots.
BOTTOM: A snake plant in a terra cotta pot.

Sometimes it is easier to break a pot to safely remove your houseplant.

moisture-loving plants such as any ferns, *Goeppertia* (formerly the *Calathea* genus), peace lilies, and others in these pots.

Terra cotta pots are much heavier than plastic and therefore are a better choice if you have any top-heavy plants.

As far as repotting goes, if I have a spe-cial plant growing in a terra cotta pot and I'm worried that I'll damage my plant by taking it out, I have no qualms about tak-ing a hammer to the pot to break the plant free. Terra cotta is inexpensive, and my plants are more important to me than sav-ing the pot.

There are quite a few disadvantages to terra cotta pots that you should be aware of. They can be pretty fragile. When you are purchasing them, inspect them carefully, because many have hairline cracks. Because they are so porous, they can allow potting mix to dry out *extremely* quickly, especially the smaller pots. I have almost stopped using 4-inch terra cotta pots because they require watering much more frequently than I like.

Since they are so porous, be careful where you set terra cotta pots. A terra cotta pot can quickly damage any wooden furniture unless you place the pot on a plastic saucer or something similar that is impermeable to water.

Terra cotta pots will also absorb many minerals from tap water as well as any fertilizer salts. These will appear as a whitish deposit on the outside of the pot. Mold can also grow on the exterior of the pot. Over time you may even have green algae or moss growing as well. I think it gives the pot a beautiful patina, but if you don't like the look of it, you may want to avoid using terra cotta pots altogether. The buildup can be easily scrubbed off however.

Finally, it helps to soak brand new terra cotta pots in warm water for about half an hour before using them. This helps condition the pot so that it doesn't wick excessive moisture out of your soil. Even after doing this, I do find that it can take a few instances of watering a plant that has been newly potted in a terra cotta pot before it stabilizes and doesn't wick excessive moisture out of the potting mix.

A blooming snake plant growing in a plastic nursery pot and slipped into a decorative pot.

Glazed Ceramic Pots

Glazed ceramic pots are available in a large and beautiful variety of colors, designs, shapes, and sizes. Because they are glazed, they will hold moisture very well. They also tend to be much more expensive than terra cotta and plastic pots. I typically use these as cachepots, especially ones that don't have a drainage hole.

RIGHT: An assortment of snake plants in various types of pots. Terra cotta pots will dry out the fastest.

POTTING MIXES

Potting mixes make up a critical aspect of houseplant health and should not be over-looked or skimmed over. There isn't *one* magic potting mix that will work for your plants. Many different mediums and mixes will work, but there are some aspects to consider.

Many blends work well, and many people have their own special recipes that they like to use. I will share with you the mixes I like to use. You can start with these, and you are welcome to tweak your blends to suit *your* growing environment! There is no need to overcomplicate the issue by making fancy homemade mixes from scratch, but there are some amend-ments that you can make to many com-mercially available all-purpose mixes that will improve them.

A good potting mix will have good mois-ture retention, but it will also have good porosity and drainage. Depending on the materials used, a potting mix can hold more or less moisture. Prepackaged all-purpose potting mixes tend to retain more mois-ture than cactus/succulent mixes, which are designed to dry out more quickly.

Depending on what I'm growing, I like to start out with an all-purpose potting mix or cactus/succulent blend and then amend those mixes by adding coarse particles such as perlite, pumice, or even orchid bark in various ratios. *I almost never use most com-mercial potting mixes as is.* In my experi-ence, most lack the required porosity that is so beneficial for growing plants indoors.

Materials such as perlite, pumice, and orchid bark, once blended into your pre-packaged potting mixes, will create many small air pockets and improve drainage. When you water your plants, those air pockets will fill with water and your plant's roots will drink it up. Once your plant uses up the water, the roots will then have oxy-gen available as a result of these air pockets.

Both perlite and pumice are wonderful soil additives that help aerate your potting mixes, prevent compaction, and improve drainage. Unlike vermiculite, neither really retain much water.

Perlite, a form of volcanic glass, is mined and then heated to the point where it essen-tially pops like popcorn, resulting in the very lightweight white particles that are incorporated into potting mixes. It is fairly inexpensive. One downside is that it tends to float to the top over time, especially if you are too vigorous with watering.

If you don't like using perlite, you can use pumice, which is a volcanic rock. It is more expensive than perlite and is not as readily available. Pumice is a heavier material, which provides more stability to a houseplant. As a result, it makes it less likely that the pot will get knocked over. Pumice also has the added benefit that it won't float to the surface like perlite tends to do. I tend to use pumice for succulents or top-heavy plants.

The trouble with many prepackaged potting mixes, when they're not amended to increase porosity, is that they tend to stay wet for too long indoors. This is because they often don't have enough chunky mate-

Perlite

Pumice

rial mixed in. I find that this is especially the case for cactus/succulent mixes. And if your soil stays wet for too long, the lack of oxygen at the root system will create conditions that can encourage root rot.

Let's say you have a plant and you are:

- repotting into a pot that is much too big for its root system
- using a potting mix that doesn't have enough porosity
- placing the plant in a dark corner in your house

Well . . . this is a perfect recipe for root rot: plants use up less water when they're in very low light. If you use a pot that is much too big for your plant, that high volume of soil will take much longer to dry out. Add to this the fact that your potting mix isn't porous, and the result is that your mix will stay wet for too long and make too little oxygen available at the root zone. This is literally a recipe for disaster.

Increasing the porosity of your soil will partly help protect against root rot. But if you can ensure that your plant is growing in decent light, you avoid placing your plant into an oversized pot, you use porous potting mixes and proper watering techniques, and you allow your soil to dry out sufficiently in between watering, root rot will be a thing of the past!

Here are some examples of blends that I use for my houseplants. Note that these work for me, but you may need to tweak them to suit your needs.

All-Purpose Tropical Foliage Mix

This is a wonderful general purpose mix for leafy tropicals. I've had great success with this simple mix:

3 parts of a peat-based potting mix
+ 1 part perlite

Perhaps you live in a very dry, hot climate and you need more moisture retention. In this case you can try:

4 parts of a peat-based potting mix
+ 1 part perlite

Aroid Mix

I've also used the following mix successfully for aroids, especially for anthuriums, monsteras, and others:

1 part peat-based potting mix + 1 part orchid bark + 1 part perlite

Succulent and Cactus Mix

This is a great mix for succulents like echeverias, aloes, and even for plants that need to dry out quickly between watering such as hoyas:

2 parts succulent and/or cactus mix
+ 1 part perlite + 1 part ¼-inch pumice

I've also used:

2 parts succulent and/or cactus mix
+ 1 part ¼-inch pumice

Keep in mind that the more additional chunky material (perlite, pumice, or orchid bark) that you add to your all-purpose potting mix, the faster your blend will dry out. You can adjust accordingly in order to suit your environmental conditions.

Blend for Self-Watering Pots

Self-watering pots need really porous mediums because your mix will stay moist. Because of this, you will need to incorporate a lot of coarse material in order to avoid root rot. This blend has worked very well in my experience:

1 part peat-based potting mix + 1 part vermiculite + 1 part perlite

You can use these mixes as a starting point. They work well for me. After you give them a try, you can make any adjustments needed. Perhaps you live in a very dry, hot climate and you need more moisture retention. In this case you can try four parts, instead of three parts, of a peat-based potting mix and one part perlite. There are many variations that will work, so experiment and see what works best for your conditions. You may even come up with your own special mix that works well with your houseplant care routine and indoor conditions.

In all cases, though, whatever you do, most prepackaged potting mixes should be amended to create more porosity. After all, healthy roots make for healthy plants.

RIGHT: An assortment of philodendron plants.

PART THREE.

How Can I Troubleshoot Plant Problems?

In this section, I outline some of the most common plant problems and provide case studies to help you identify where you might be going wrong in your plant care. When trying to determine what caused a particular plant issue, whether it is yellow leaves, crispy brown edges on leaves, wilting, or a host of other plant woes, you'll always hear me say to physically observe your plant and be aware of your conditions and routines. I've seen so many plant parents struggle because they blindly believe statements they've read on the internet.

LEFT: Brown edges on a cast-iron plant leaf
resulting from very dry potting mix.
RIGHT: Healthy cast-iron plant leaves.

In order to be successful, you must be *open to adapting*. If you are plagued with plant woes but aren't changing anything you are doing, you can't possibly expect to have different results. Be bold and *make a change*.

The important thing to keep in mind is that all of our plant woes can be caused by a variety of different things, and you have to be an active plant parent and physically observe your indoor conditions to determine the cause. This requires asking yourself many questions.

Because of my analytical problem-solving background, this comes naturally to me. I've been able to help many people drill down into the causes of their plant problems. When approached by a frantic plant parent, I often need to act as a therapist to console the distressed party first and then act as a problem solver to determine what went wrong.

The following cases represent conversations I've had while helping my readers with their problems. I've highlighted these because they are the most frequent problems that plant parents have, especially newer plant parents.

These case studies also give you examples of questions to ask yourself in various scenarios. My goal is to teach you to ask yourself the right questions so that you can eventually help yourself and diagnose exactly what happened, with aplomb!

Approach any issues with an open mind, and don't forget to be kind to yourself throughout the process. Troubleshooting takes time and experience, but you, too, can learn to do it effectively!

Key 6.

What Thought Process Should I Use to Fix Common Plant Problems?

COMMON PLANT PROBLEMS

Brown Tips

Many things can cause brown tips, so it is important to observe *why* they occurred. Although low humidity can cause brown tips in some cases, in the vast majority of cases it is likely due to soil moisture issues.

If your potting mix has gone completely dry, many plants will respond with dry, crispy leaf edges. Even the entire leaf might show signs of distress, especially moisture-loving plants like peace lily, *Goeppertia* (formerly known as *Calathea*), and ferns. Feel your potting mix with your finger. Is it really dry? Lift your pot. Does it feel really light?

If you keep your potting mix too wet and root rot starts to set in, your plant can no longer take in water through its roots. This essentially (and ironically) causes the leaves to dehydrate and you can get brown tips as well. If the root rot is bad enough, your entire plant can also start to wilt. Feel your potting mix. Has it stayed wet for a while? Is the plant sitting in water?

If your plant is severely root-bound, it is probably drying out very quickly. Often, it is hard to keep a plant with this condition adequately watered, and thus your plant

This peace lily has developed brown leaf tips from repeatedly drying out too much.

isn't getting all the water that it really needs. This can also cause brown tips and edges on your leaves.

Overfertilization is another reason for brown leaf edges. Remember that less is more when you're fertilizing! *Always* measure both your fertilizer and water. If you eyeball either amount, it can result in an overly concentrated solution that can burn your plants, especially more sensitive ones.

Do you bottom water? If you're not periodically top watering with plain water, you could be getting a buildup of minerals or salts in your potting mix from tap water or fertilizer. As it builds up, you can get brown tips. Many times, you will see a white or even brownish or gray crusty buildup on the surface of the potting mix

Healthy peace lily

or even on the rim of a pot. These are built-up salts.

Some houseplants are reportedly sensitive to fluoride in tap water. Corn plants (*Dracaena* genus) and spider plants (*Chlorophytum comosum*) are notoriously said to be sensitive to fluoride. Plants in the prayer plant family, peace lily (*Spathiphyllum*), *Yucca*, or cast-iron plant (*Aspidistra*) are also reportedly sensitive to fluoride. If you are confident that you have good conditions for your plant and still have brown tips, try experimenting with your water sources for these plants. Use rain water, distilled, or filtered water for a period of time and see if you notice a difference. Note that any leaves that have browned will *not* turn green again. You'll have to monitor the new growth over time to see the true effect.

Several yellow leaves developed on this croton after the potting mix dried out completely for too long.

Yellow Leaves

There are a tremendous number of reasons why your plant may have yellow leaves. A potting mix that is too dry can cause yellow leaves, but so can a potting mix that stays wet for too long. Cold temperatures, nutrient deficiencies (although this is not as common), too little light, and even too much light can also cause yellow leaves.

When you read information online that says something like, "Yellow leaves are caused by soil that stays too wet," keep in mind that this is only *one* possible reason and that there are many others, as you've just seen.

If your potting mix has gone completely dry for too long, it is common for the lower leaves of your plant to turn yellow. Does your pothos, monstera, or philodendron have a yellow leaf? As soon as you notice this, feel the soil with your finger. Is it completely dry? Does the pot feel light? When was the last time you watered? Yellow leaves can happen even with succulents. They still need water! Although it is beneficial for them to dry out completely, if you wait too long, they will also reach their breaking point.

If you notice yellow leaves and you feel your potting mix and it's wet (even though it hasn't been watered in a while), try and determine why. Does your pot not have a drainage hole and you slipped and added too much water one day (no drainage means that water has nowhere to go!)?

Healthy croton

Perhaps the pot has a drainage hole, but you let the water drain into its saucer and it sat in water for a while. Or maybe your plant is growing in a plastic nursery container with drainage holes, but you placed it in a decorative pot with no drainage. And when you water, you never check to see if water accumulates in the decorative pot.

I Didn't Change Anything, Why Is My Plant Suffering All of a Sudden?

Have you had a houseplant that was thriving for a while and then, seemingly out of the blue, it started to get excessive yellow leaves, brown leaves, or worse? If so, you might be telling yourself, "I don't under-stand! I haven't changed a *thing,* and it was doing so well for a long time!"

Remember that just because *you* haven't changed anything, that doesn't mean your plant hasn't! Your plant has grown. Maybe it has gotten excessively root-bound. This is when you have to be a flexible plant parent. If your plant has slowly become very root-bound, yet you still maintain the "once a week" watering schedule, your plant will eventually suffer because it will be dry-ing out much more quickly than it used to. Try and be flexible with your watering and not stick to a rigid schedule, because *plants change* even if you don't!

Root Rot

The dreaded root rot! If your plant stays in wet soil for very long periods of time, its roots will literally suffocate. Waterlogged potting mixes, especially ones that don't have any coarse materials mixed in, will have little to no oxygen and produce anaer-obic conditions (lack of oxygen) that will make plants prone to pathogens, which will rot out the roots.

Some symptoms of root rot include wilting of the entire plant and very poor growth. The soil may even smell rancid in really bad cases. In addition, you may notice that your plant perhaps has been sitting in water and your potting mix stayed too wet for too long.

To know for sure if your plant has suf-fered from root rot, you'll have to actually observe the roots. Take your plant out of its pot and inspect the roots. A plant that has suffered from root rot will typically have developed darker colored, mushy roots. If the roots feel dry and brittle, there is no root rot.

If you suspect root rot, there are a few things that you can try to help the plant (if the root rot is not in its advanced stages). Immediately discard any excess water that your plant may be sitting in. If your plant is in a darker location, move it to brighter light. Don't water the plant until the soil has dried out. If this doesn't seem to improve the situation, you can always try to propagate your plant so that you can start from scratch.

Plants That Look Pale

Do you have any houseplants that seem to have lost their coloration and look pale? Check your soil immediately if you see this. Chances are good that the soil will be quite dry. From personal experience, I've noticed that the following plants will go very pale and appear discolored when the potting mix stays dry for too long: spider plants, ferns, and some begonias (especially *Begonia maculata*).

Phototropism

This is simply a fancy word that means a plant is growing toward a light source. Indoors, this is very common because, in most cases, there is light coming in from only one direction (through a window). Outdoors, plants receive light from many directions, so it's much less pronounced in most cases.

Do you have a houseplant with leaves that are mostly leaning or reaching for a window? The traditional advice has been to give your plant a quarter turn every time you water in order to encourage balanced growth. If, like me, you have a lot of plants, this can be a pain.

I simply turn my plants 180 degrees anytime I see phototropism in action. I regularly rotate my *Pilea peperomioides* this way so that the plant grows more symmetrically.

Variegated Plants Going All Green or All Variegated

Do you have a variegated plant that suddenly reverted back to all green leaves? Or perhaps the opposite happened, where it grew all white leaves, like the variegated *Monstera deliciosa* plants often do. The Philodendron 'Pink Princess' may produce leaves that are fully pink. These all-white or all-pink leaves have no chlorophyll in them, and although they are very pretty, they won't last forever.

To keep more balanced variegation in your plant, you'll want to cut off the all-green leaves (or on the opposite end, the all-white leaves, in the case of a variegated monstera, or all pink leaves in the case of Philodendron 'Pink Princess'). Start at the tip of the plant and work your way down. Cut the vine back to the first leaf that exhibits a balanced variegation. The resulting growth should exhibit more balanced variegation.

A healthy Chinese evergreen.

Smaller Leaves on Newer Growth

Does new growth have smaller leaves than the rest of the plant? This is probably a sign that you should increase the light for your plant. Other cultural shortcomings could be the culprit, such as the soil having been dried out for too long.

Also keep in mind that the new leaves that result from plants growing in our homes may be smaller than those leaves that grew when the plant was in the greenhouse. Indoor conditions at home are inferior to those of a greenhouse, so we have to manage our expectations.

PESTS

Whether we like it or not, pests are part of growing houseplants. We all get them sooner or later. Healthy plants will be much less prone to insect attacks. Stressed plants, however, will be very prone to insect attacks. Among the most common indoor plant pests include aphids, fungus gnats, mealybugs, spider mites, scale, and thrips.

Aphids

Aphids are soft-bodied insects that are typically up to $\frac{1}{8}$ inch in size. Most of the aphids that I've seen are green, but they can come in a variety of colors, including yellow and black. You will typically find aphids feeding on the new growth of your plants. As they suck the sap out of your plant, you will often see deformed growth. Along with the aphids themselves, you will also see a sticky and shiny material on your plant called honeydew. The honeydew is a waste product of the aphids, and if left for a while, it will also have sooty mold growing on top of it that appears dark.

On top of all this, aphids can also transmit plant viruses. If you have aphids, the first thing you can do to control them is to simply take your plant to a sink or shower and knock the pests off with a spray of water. If it's warm outside, you can easily do this with a hose. This may be sufficient to control them. You can also use various sprays including insecticidal soap, horticultural oil, or neem oil.

Fungus Gnats

If you see little black flies flying around your plants, they are likely fungus gnats. In small numbers, they're more of an annoyance to people than anything. But if you have a large infestation, it *can* be a big problem for both you and your plants!

Fungus gnat larvae live in the top portion of your plant's potting mix, where they feed on organic matter and fungi in the soil, hence their name. The larvae thrive in moist soil, so if you tend to keep your potting mixes too wet, you are greatly perpetuating the issue by doing so, not to mention increasing your chances of root rot!

Yellow sticky traps are helpful for controlling the adult fungus gnats. The adult

Adult fungus gnats that were captured on a yellow sticky trap.

fungus gnats will be attracted to them and literally fly into the traps and be stuck there. Trapping the adults will prevent them from laying eggs in your potting mix.

To prevent fungus gnat issues before they start, allow the top inch or so of your soil to dry out. This will help greatly. Prevention is the best way to control them!

In the meantime, if you have a more severe infestation, products such as Mosquito Bits and Gnatrol use a naturally occurring bacteria called BTI. Adding these products to your potting mix will kill the larvae. If you kill the larvae, they won't progress into adult gnats that will then, in turn, lay more eggs and perpetuate the cycle.

If you don't want to use a product with

BTI, systemic houseplant insecticides are also very effective for killing fungus gnat larvae. One product that I use is Bonide's Systemic Houseplant Insect Control Granules, and it is very effective against a variety of pests. You simply add it to your potting mix and water your plant, and the pesticide is absorbed by the roots, protecting the entire plant from the inside out.

Mealybugs

Mealybugs are white, cottony looking insects that you can potentially find in every nook and cranny of your plant. When they are small, they look like white specks. Like aphids, they suck on the sap of your plants and also cause deformed growth. Also like aphids, they excrete honeydew.

To control mealybugs, a traditional

Mealy bug on a jade plant.

method is to dip a Q-tip in 70 percent rubbing alcohol (isopropyl alcohol) and rub it on each mealybug. This will kill them on contact. But where there is one mealybug, there will be others lurking. You can also make a 50/50 mix of water and 70 percent isopropyl alcohol to use as a spray. Some people dilute it further, but I've found this ratio is safe for most plants. If you are concerned, you can test a small area and monitor it over a day or two. If all is okay, then you can spray the whole plant.

You can also spray with insecticidal soap, horticultural oil, or neem oil.

Spider Mites

Spider mites can be harder to detect because they are very small. They are actually not true insects at all, but are more closely related to spiders. These are also sap-sucking pests, and the presence of fine webbing on your plant is a telltale sign that you have spider mites. Often, the leaves will have a mottled appearance and will be discolored or yellowish.

To deal with spider mite infestations, I like to first rinse the entire plant off very well, including the undersides of the leaves. For larger-leaved plants, sometimes I also wipe the top and bottom of the leaves with a damp paper towel. You will often see a yellowish residue that wipes off.

After this, you can spray with an insecticidal soap, horticultural oil, or neem oil.

Spider mites thrive in warm conditions and dry air. If you have any plants that are prone to spider mites, it is helpful to occasionally mist them to help deter this pest.

Scale

Unlike all the other pests detailed here, the adult scale does not move. Only in what is called the crawler stage will scale move around. They eventually settle on a spot on your plant, where they attach and feed on your plant's sap. They will then mature and develop a brownish-colored shell. Left unchecked, like many pests, they can become a huge problem. Early detection, followed by treatment, is always helpful.

Here is my process that I use to deal with scale. First, I physically inspect the entire plant, including the underside of leaves, stems, leaf axils, and so on. I like to physically remove these pests first with my fingers. If you do the same, be sure to check the undersides of the leaves as they often are lurking there. In tighter areas that are

Scale and honeydew on a phalaenopsis orchid.

difficult or awkward to reach with my fingers, such as the leaf axils and petioles, I sometimes use a toothpick to dislodge and remove the scale. It is important to physically remove every visible scale because, oftentimes, sprays will not work on the armored scale's dome, which is hard and waxy.

Next, I rinse off the plant in a sink or shower. This helps wash away any scale that is still too small to see with the naked eye. It also helps clean up any honeydew that the scale excreted on the plant. Soft scale insects secrete honeydew, but the harder shelled scale do not.

Next, I like to spray the plant with an insecticidal soap. Complete coverage is *very* important, so I spray the entire plant until it is dripping. All surfaces including the undersides of the leaves need to be sprayed. You can also use a horticultural oil as well. As an added precaution, I like to also apply a systemic insecticide onto the soil and water it in, like previously described. The insecticide gets absorbed by the plant through its roots and protects the plant from the inside out.

A week later, I'll inspect the plant again, remove any new scale that I may have missed or that developed, and spray again. I continue to monitor closely and repeat spraying as needed to control and/or eliminate the scale.

Thrips

Thrips are very small pests and are difficult to see. The immature nymphs and adults both suck out plant sap. Leaves that have

Thrips on a *Peperomia polybotrya*.

Pest Control Best Practices

- Prevention and early action are key in pest control. The earlier you can spot and treat pests, the easier it will be to manage them. Pests are inevitable and contending with them is a part of being a plant parent.
- If you use any spray applications (insecticidal soap, horticultural oil, neem oil, and so forth), it is important to get total coverage on your plant and spray to the point of dripping. Don't just spray where you saw the pest. Oftentimes, the eggs and larvae will be difficult or impossible to see with the naked eye, so every surface of the plant must be sprayed.
- Keep up spraying for at least a week or two after you don't notice the pests anymore. This will ensure that you've taken care of what isn't easily visible.
- For your safety, always use any pest treatment according to the directions on the label.

been attacked by thrips often appear speckled. These pests can be among the most challenging to deal with, but fortunately they are less commonly seen than pests like mealybugs and scale. Thrips are weak flyers, and often if you disturb the leaves, you'll see them quickly hop away. Adults are slender and appear dark, whereas the nymphs are paler in color.

The first thing I do to treat thrips is to spray down the entire plant with water in the sink or the shower, or even outside if I can. If I can't do this, I wipe down the leaves with a damp paper towel or cloth. Then I treat the entire plant with insecticidal soap or horticultural oil. It may require multiple applications. These are very persistent pests, so you have to be even more persistent!

A healthy, pest-free fern.

Case Studies

The following case studies are all based on actual problems my readers experienced and approached me about. Many of the same problems kept cropping up over and over again, so I've summarized both the problem and the thought process with the resolution in the five different cases.

In each case, an incorrect assumption was made, but in the end, a physical observation and some critical thinking saved the day.

CASE #1: The assumption of a "rotting" snake plant.

CASE #2: The assumption of an "underwatered" pothos developing yellow leaves.

CASE #3: The assumption of an "overwatered" peace lily that is wilting.

CASE #4: The assumption of a monstera not growing because of a lack of fertilizer.

BONUS CASE: My string of pearls looks like it has bleached out.

Each case speaks for itself. Hopefully you will be able to relate it to a similar problem you might have!

CASE #1:
THE ASSUMPTION OF A ROTTING SNAKE PLANT

Plant Parent: Help! My snake plant is rotting because I overwatered. What can I do to help it?

Me: How do you know it rotted? Are you sure you overwatered? Can you feel your soil right now and tell me if it's dry or wet?

Plant Parent: The leaves look wrinkly and even started to yellow a bit. I read somewhere that this means it was overwatered and started to rot, so that's why I said that. Actually, now that I felt the soil, it feels really dry.

Me: How do you water? Tell me your routine?

Plant Parent: I know they are sensitive to overwatering, so I add two tablespoons of water every other week.

Me: Have you done this as long as you've had this plant?

Plant Parent: Yes.

Me: Based on what I have heard, your plant is not rotting at all. It has been weakened from too little watering, and you've actually dehydrated your plant's roots, which is the opposite of rotting. By only watering with two tablespoons of water, you're not thoroughly moistening your potting media and therefore you've completely dried out and damaged much of the root system. And if you have a weak root system, you will have a weak plant. You should always thoroughly water all your houseplants, regardless of whether you have a snake plant or a fern.

You're right to consider your plant's sensitivity to staying too wet. But rather than varying the amount of water you use when watering, you should vary how dry you allow the potting mix to become in between watering. For snake plants, you want them to dry out almost completely or completely. Some plants, like ferns, do like to be watered as soon as the surface starts to dry out, but snake plants like to dry out all the way. So go ahead and give your plant a thorough watering, let excess water escape the drainage hole, and repeat this process when the potting mix goes completely dry again. Know that it will take some time for your plant to recover, though.

Plant Parent: Thank you so much! This has been so helpful!

Additional Commentary: A Lesson in Observation

I know, I'm talking about overwatering again! I can't tell you how many times people have told me they thought that they have overwatered. It's important to remember that you simply can't determine the cause of a plant issue without physically observing your plant. When people approach me with their plant problems, the first thing I ask them to do is to actually *feel the plant's soil* with their finger. The plant parent is almost always shocked to discover that the soil is dry even though they thought they overwatered. All too often this is the result of blindly trusting a search on the internet.

In this case, the plant parent made two assumptions: the first was that the plant was rotting, and the second was that overwatering caused the rotting. Upon understanding all the details of care and observing the plant's physical state, it was clear to me that neither of these assumptions were true and that the plant was essentially suffering from dehydration.

If the plant had truly suffered from root rot, the only way to know for sure would have been to take the plant out of its pot and inspect the roots. Roots that have rotted out will typically be a darker color, as well as soft and mushy.

CASE #2: THE ASSUMPTION OF AN UNDERWATERED POTHOS DEVELOPING YELLOW LEAVES

Plant Parent: Help! My pothos has a bunch of yellow leaves because I think I underwatered. What can I do to help it?

Me: Tell me about your watering routine.

Plant Parent: I haven't watered it in a few weeks, and I read online that they should be watered once a week, so that's why I feel like it has been underwatered. How can I save it?

Me: Can you go ahead and stick your finger in the potting mix and tell me if it's wet or dry?

Plant Parent: It feels wet. Now I'm confused.

Me: Can you send me a photo of your plant?

Plant Parent: Sure.

Me: (*After viewing the photo.*) It looks like you have your pothos growing in a plastic pot and it's slipped into a decorative ceramic pot.

Plant Parent: Yes, that's right.

Me: I assume that your plastic pot has drainage holes and the ceramic pot does not?

Plant Parent: Correct.

Me: Based off what I've heard, I bet your plant is sitting in water. Can you lift your plastic pot with the plant out of the ceramic pot and tell me what you see?

Plant Parent: Oh wow, there is a bunch of water sitting there.

Me: Your plant has been getting yellow leaves because it has stayed wet for weeks due to sitting in excess water, even though you haven't watered in weeks.

Plant Parent: Now that I think about it, when I first got the plant, I think I added a lot of water the first time I watered it.

Me: There you go! You should *always* water your plants thoroughly, but all the excess has to drain away. Go ahead and dump the excess water out of the decorative pot. If you water your plant in place, always lift the plant out of the decorative pot and dump out any excess water. Or, simply take the plant out of its pot, water it in a sink or shower, let the water finish draining, and then place it back inside the decorative pot.

Additional Commentary: A Lesson in Multiple Causes of Yellowing Leaves

This plant parent incorrectly determined that she was underwatering her plant simply because she hasn't watered in weeks. In reality, the problem was more complex than that: overly moist soil due to a poor drainage system. If you remember from the watering section of Key 4 (page 50), you shouldn't definitively determine when to water based on a schedule. This plant parent was relying on a schedule without actually observing her potting mix and drainage system.

This is a perfect example of how one specific issue, like yellowing leaves, can be caused by a variety of factors. As we saw in Case #1, yellow leaves can also be a result of your potting mix going completely dry. Pothos will readily get yellow leaves if they are allowed to stay completely dry for too long, but here the plant parent had the opposite problem. If you've moved your plant to an area that has much less light, or if you live in an area where winter days are short and dark, your plant might form yellow leaves. So let your observations help you find a balance.

CASE #3:
THE ASSUMPTION OF AN "OVERWATERED" PEACE LILY THAT IS WILTING

Plant Parent: My peace lily is wilting because I overwatered. How can I help it?

Me: How do you know that you overwatered?

Plant Parent: I read online that wilting peace lilies mean that overwatering happened.

Me: Did you feel your potting mix?

Plant Parent: No, I just assumed the source I read was right.

Me: Go ahead and feel your potting mix and tell me if it's dry or wet.

Plant Parent: Hm, it actually feels really dry.

Me: So your source was correct in that peace lilies *can* wilt if you keep them too wet for too long, but they also do the same thing when they go too dry. You just felt the soil and observed that it was bone dry. Go ahead and take your plant to the sink and give it a good drench. You may have to soak it a few times if the potting medium got super dry. Your plant will recover over the next few hours.

Plant Parent: Wow, thank you so much! You've been a great help.

Additional Commentary: A Lesson on Using the Internet to Make a Diagnosis

Just as with yellowing leaves, there can be many causes for wilting plants. Our plant parent here made the mistake of diagnosing the problem based on a quick internet search, but, as we've learned, only in-person observations can really tell you what's wrong with your foliage—and a lot can go wrong to cause wilting. For example, peace lilies that have been kept dry will eventually collapse and wilt. As long as you don't wait too long after they have collapsed, they will quickly come back when you water thoroughly.

On the other hand, plants can also wilt

and collapse from root rot, which can happen if they stay excessively wet for too long. Ironically, if your plant is starting to suffer from root rot, it technically is being dehydrated. This seems counterintuitive, right? Because the roots are rotting and dying, the plant has no way to take in water through the roots anymore, and therefore the plant is wilting because it can no longer take up water properly.

CASE #4: THE ASSUMPTION OF A MONSTERA NOT GROWING BECAUSE OF LACK OF FERTILIZING

Plant Parent: How did you get your monstera so big! It's beautiful! Mine isn't growing at all. I started fertilizing but it still isn't doing anything.

Me: How far is your plant from a window?

Plant Parent: It's a few feet, I think. It seems pretty bright in there. It is still all green and looks healthy, but it just hasn't grown at all.

Me: Can you measure exactly how far your monstera is from your window?

Plant Parent: It's about 10 feet from my window. There is only one window in the room.

Me: What exposure is that window?

Plant Parent: It faces north.

Me: I can say with 100 percent certainty that you need to move your plant right in front of that window. Light intensity diminishes very rapidly the farther you move away from your windows. Move it right in front of your window, or better yet, if you have a larger window somewhere else, move it there. That will help too. Eastern windows would be a great window for that plant. Morning sunshine is beneficial for virtually all plants indoors. Keep it as close to the window as you can without actually touching the window. Give it a little time, and you should start to see a big difference in the growth of your plant. Light is the most important aspect of plant growth. Adding fertilizer is not a substitute for poor cultural conditions.

Plant Parent: Thanks! This helps a ton!

Additional Commentary: A Lesson on the Importance of Light

As you read in Key 1 (page 20), light is important to the growth of *all* plants, and low-light houseplants can still benefit from some sunshine. Our plant parent here underestimated the importance of light and jumped to conclusions about fertilizer before considering the plant's positioning in the home. This is another lesson in avoiding assumptions and taking all factors into account before diagnosing a plant problem.

When faced with stunted growth or slow growth, remember that light is the most important aspect of plant growth, period. You will always have better success by keeping your plants as close to windows as possible, as long as you don't go too far in the opposite direction and give your plant too much light. It's also helpful to consider your specific orientation to the sun when positioning your plant. As our plant parent here experienced, windows with a northern exposure (in the Northern Hemisphere) have the least amount of light. That, coupled with the plant being 10 feet away from the window, created very dim conditions. As for regular fertilization, it should be a complement to good cultural conditions and should not be used as a replacement.

BONUS CASE: WHY DOES MY STRING OF PEARLS LOOK LIKE IT HAS BLEACHED OUT?

Plant Parent: My string of pearls plant has turned white, almost like it burned, but I'm not sure why.

Me: Tell me how you care for the plant. Has anything changed at all? Did you do anything differently?

Plant Parent: It's been right in front of an eastern-facing window. I've had it there for a few months and it has been perfectly fine and healthy! I water thoroughly only after the potting mix has dried out completely. I'm not sure what happened.

Me: Did you just notice the bleached-out leaves?

Plant Parent: Yes, it seemed to happen pretty suddenly.

Me: Are you sure you didn't change anything? Did you move the plant recently, even for a little while?

Plant Parent: Actually, I had read that these plants like sun, so I took the plant outside and it spent the entire day in full sun. It didn't seem to like that, because I noticed some of the pearls appeared whitish and bleached-out, so I got scared and moved it from the eastern window over to a north window where it doesn't get any direct sun now.

Me: You're right, these plants love direct sun! But it sounds like the issue that you have is that you didn't properly acclimate your plant to higher light levels. The intensity of light outdoors is much higher than indoors. If you wanted to keep your plant outdoors in the sun, you would need to gradually increase the light, otherwise it will burn. For example, you'd have to place your plant in full shade outdoors for a while. Only at that point could you start to introduce some direct sun. From there, you'd increase any direct sun slowly and gradually. Think of it this way: if you had very fair skin and were indoors all winter and then decided to go on a beach vacation to Mexico, if you didn't get a little base tan first (and wear some sunscreen), you would very quickly burn. Plants are not that different!

Plant Parent: Wow, I didn't know that! Thank you! I'll be aware of that for the next time I move any plants outside.

Additional Commentary: A Lesson in Increasing Light Too Abruptly

This plant parent initially had the right idea about her plant's preferences: string of pearls *do* like direct sun. But a hasty move to the outdoors led her to mistakenly conclude that her string of pearls didn't like direct sun because her plant burned when she took it outside. The fact is that even plants that *do* like direct sun need some acclimation to brighter light, and this needs to be done slowly. Any plant will burn if you suddenly increase the intensity of its light exposure.

PART FOUR.

How Can I Easily Make More Plants?

Part of the fun of growing houseplants is learning how to propagate them. Propagation is simply the process of creating new plants. Whether you want to increase your own collection or share with family and friends, propagating your plants is fun and there are many ways to do it.

A variegated monstera that was propagated in water and later planted in this pot with a moss pole.

In the following chapter, I discuss some of the most common ways to propagate houseplants. There are even more methods than those that I discuss in this book, but the ones I've included will give you plenty to experiment with—not to mention plenty of new plants!

Once you learn these methods, you can apply them to many other plants, even ones that are not listed in this book. For some plants, all you'll need is a single leaf. For others, you'll need a bit more of the plant; I'll explain everything here. Some plants propagate much more readily than others, while some will take their grand old time.

I make note of approximately how long you can expect to wait so you have an idea, and I also discuss what conditions are beneficial in order to shorten the propagation time. Propagation time can vary quite drastically depending on your conditions (light, temperature, etc.).

LEFT: Snake plant leaf cutting with pups.

Key 7.

What Methods Can I Use to Propagate?

There are myriad ways to propagate plants and it is really fun to experiment in order to increase your own collection, or to share with fellow houseplant enthusiasts. This chapter focuses on some vegetative propagation methods (using stems, roots, and leaves) that you can easily employ at home, along with illustrated examples of various houseplants.

There are many more ways to propagate, but hopefully this will spark your interest in the topic and you can continue to experiment, learn on your own, and have fun!

The following basic vegetative propagation methods will be described:

DIVISION: This is the quickest method to propagate, which is great if you're impatient, but it can be used only if your plant has multiple stems or multiple crowns. You simply divide the plant at the root system, pot the parts up, and you instantly have new plants.

Take your plant out of the pot. Then either tease the roots gently apart with your hands, or if that's too difficult, take a knife and cut straight through the root ball, making sure that each section of the plant has roots attached. Don't worry, you will not harm your plant!

On the next page are some aloe pups that were all in the same pot. I simply took them out of the pot and gently separated each individual plant and potted them up separately. Since it was a neglected plant, the root systems were not very vigorous so it was easy to divide.

CUTTINGS: This is the most popular method to propagate: you simply sever pieces of a stem or vine, or in some cases, take leaf cuttings. You then place the cuttings in water or straight into a potting mix. A period of rooting occurs before the plant's growth starts to take off.

Aloe pups that were divided and are ready to pot up.

PROPAGATION WITH STEM CUTTINGS

Many plants, particularly plants in the Aroid family (see Araceae Family of Plants on page 126 for examples of these plants), are easily propagated by placing stem cuttings in water. You'll want to make sure the cutting includes a node (where the leaf and petiole meets the stem), as this is where growth will occur. In many cases, you can already see an aerial root growing on the node. An aerial root is simply a root that is growing above ground or not in potting mix.

Leaf

Petiole

Node

A rooted single-node leaf cutting of pothos. You can clearly see that both the roots and a new shoot is growing from the node.

A hanging basket of pothos that I created using a couple dozen single-node cuttings.

Be sure to change the water frequently, at least once a week, to keep it clean and fresh. If you see anything rotting, or notice any cloudy water, remove any debris and replace with clean, fresh water.

Pothos can easily be propagated in this manner. You can maximize your cuttings by utilizing single node cuttings. Simply snip the vine on either size of the node (where the petiole meets the vine).

Each cutting will grow a vine. If you want a very full plant, include multiple cuttings in the same container once you pot them up into potting mix.

Similar to the pothos cutting, here is another example with a *Monstera deli-ciosa* var. *borsigiana albo-variegata* that was rooted in water. Be sure to include a node or you will not get any roots.

Here is another example of a jewel orchid (*Ludisia discolor*) cutting that is placed in water to root.

You can plant any rooted cuttings directly into potting mix as soon as the roots are about an inch long or so. Don't wait terribly long, otherwise the transition will be a bit more difficult for the plant. You can also skip rooting the cuttings in water and, instead, plant them directly in potting mix. Make sure to keep the soil moist for the best results.

A water-propagated variegated monstera.

A water-propagated jewel orchid (*Ludisia discolor*) that was rooted in water.

Stem Cutting Propagation of "String of . . ." Plants

Many "string of . . ." plants (such as string of pearls, string of bananas, string of hearts, and similar plants) can easily be propagated simply by cutting off a long stem and coiling it around on the surface of some potting mix. For these plants, I like to use half succulent potting mix and half pumice as the potting medium.

When you lay them on top of the potting mix make sure that they have good contact with it. Keep your potting mix relatively moist to encourage rooting. As soon as the surface feels dry, be sure to water.

Under good light, warm temperatures, and attention to watering, here is the result about three months later.

Stem Cutting Propagation of Succulents

If you have any succulents that have lost a lot of leaves or have gotten leggy with age and you want to rejuvenate them, you can simply take a stem cutting of the leafy tip and make a new plant.

Carefully use a razor or sharp knife that has been sterilized with alcohol to make a nice clean cut. Allow the cutting to air-dry

A strand of string of bananas coiled on top of potting mix to root.

The same string of bananas plant three months later. Under good light, warmer temperatures and attention to watering, the growth was quite rapid.

for a few days, or even a week, so that the cut dries out and callouses over.

Next, dip the end that was cut into a rooting hormone if you'd like (this is helpful but not required), and insert the cutting directly into a small pot filled with potting mix. Water it well and wait until the surface of the mix dries out before watering again.

Anytime you make a cutting of any succulent, be sure to allow it to air-dry for a few days to allow the cut to callous over. This helps prevent rotting when you plant it.

PROPAGATION WITH LEAF CUTTINGS

Some plants can be propagated by single leaves. These include rex begonias, ZZ plants, snake plants, jade plants, burro's tail, and quite a few other succulents. Here are some illustrated examples.

Leaf Cutting Propagation of the Snake Plant

Snake plants can be propagated easily (though very slowly) with leaf cuttings. Simply take a leaf and cut it into several segments. Make each segment about 3 to 4 inches long. You can use a whole leaf for the propagation, but the more segments you cut, the more pups that will grow.

Let each cutting air-dry for a couple of days to help prevent rotting and then place them in water, or directly into a potting mix, to root.

Note that if you take multiple cuttings off one leaf, you *must* keep the orientation the same as how it was growing on the plant. If you turn the cuttings upside down, they will not root. One thing I like to do is to cut a V-shaped notch at the bottom of each cutting. This creates more surface area for the growing roots and pups, and it serves as a visual signal so I know which end goes into the water or potting mix.

If you choose water propagation, place the cuttings in a container of water with about 1 inch of water or so. Make sure to change the water frequently. You may also notice that your leaf cuttings will get slimy.

Water-propagated snake plant leaf cuttings that are just starting to grow roots.

Check on your cuttings a couple of times per week, and clean the cuttings under running water in a sink. Gently remove the slime with your fingers under running water. This will help prevent rotting.

Roots will form first on the leaf cuttings and then you will notice pups starting to grow.

After a few months or so, you will have perfectly developed little pups.

The fun part is that you can cut one long leaf into several segments and each one will produce pups! This leaf was cut into nine segments and each one produced pups.

Once the pups start growing, you will see that they will grow their own roots. I like to wait until the pups are about 2 or 3 inches long and have some of their own

Water-propagated snake plant leaf cuttings with roots and new pups developing.

Nicely developed pups on water-propagated snake plant leaf cuttings.

roots before I cut them off the leaf cutting and pot them up.

After I cut off the initial pups, I like to place the original leaf cutting back in water because it often continues to grow pups!

Please note that variegated cultivars may not come true if you propagate them using this leaf cutting method. This means that the resulting pups will not exhibit the same variegation as the original plant and will revert back to a more plain version.

You can cut a single snake plant leaf into multiple cuttings, and each segment will produce roots and pups.

Leaf Cutting Propagation of the ZZ Plant

Like snake plant leaf cuttings, ZZ plant propagation by single leaves, although extremely easy to do, is an exercise in patience, as it can take many months in average conditions to grow an actual plant.

Simply snip a few healthy leaves off your plant. Then place the cuttings either in water (this is fun because you can watch the growth of the rhizome) or directly into potting mix. I've done both successfully.

For propagation in potting mix, simply insert the leaf at a 45-degree angle about ½ inch deep in the potting mix in a small pot. The end of the leaf that was snipped off the plant will be the part that is buried in the potting mix. I like to use half all-purpose potting mix and half perlite for the mix. You need to keep the potting mix moist for best results. As soon as I notice the surface has dried out, I'll water.

For water propagation, simply place the leaves in a small vessel of water. The end of the leaf that was snipped off the plant should be under water. Maintain about half an inch of water or so, but keep an eye on the water level and top off with water as it evaporates.

Once you notice the rhizome starting to grow, go ahead and plant the cutting in potting mix. In time, you'll see new shoots emerging, but be patient. This entire process can take many months! Setting your propagations on a heating mat will greatly speed up the process.

A water-propagated ZZ plant leaf that is growing a rhizome.

A soil-propagated ZZ plant leaf that is starting to grow a new shoot.

Leaf Cutting Propagation
of the Jade Plant

Many succulents propagate readily just from simple leaf cuttings. Propagation in general is best done during the active growing season. Other than jade plants, you can also easily propagate some echeverias and sedums, among others, this way. Not every succulent will be able to propagate with this method, but don't be afraid to experiment!

When you take a leaf cutting, gently twist the leaf off the stem and make sure it pulls away cleanly off the stem. Be sure to take multiple leaf cuttings if you can, as not all of them may make it.

Next, lay the leaves on a flat surface in a bright location, but not in an excessively sunny location, or under a grow light. I set my jade leaves under grow lights right on my desk without potting mix! After a few weeks, the leaves start growing roots and little pups.

You can also lay the leaves flat right on top of a pot filled with potting mix. For succulent propagation, I like to use a 50/50 mix of succulent mix and perlite. You can use pumice instead of perlite if you prefer.

After you take the leaf cuttings, let them dry out for two to three days so each cut callouses over. Then simply set them flat on top of a little pot filled with potting mix. Moisten the surface of the potting mix with a spray bottle filled with water. When the surface is dry to touch, water again.

Regardless which of the two methods you choose, after the leaf cuttings start to grow roots and pups, go ahead and rest

Jade plant leaf cuttings with roots and small pups.

Jade plant leaf cuttings with pups that are starting to grow.

Jade plant leaf cuttings with pups that are ready to plant in individual pots.

them at a 45-degree angle so that the end of the leaf that is growing in contact with the potting mix and the leaf itself is supported by the rim of the pot. You can also use plastic carryout containers instead of pots.

At this stage, it is important to keep the potting mix relatively moist. Allow the surface to dry out, but then water. Small succulent plants need more water than you'd think. When the plant is much bigger and more mature, you can allow the potting mix to dry out more in between watering.

Once the pups have at least a couple of sets of leaves, and you can comfortably handle them, go ahead and transplant them wherever you want them to grow.

PART FIVE.

What Plants Should I Add to My Collection?

Although I can't possibly discuss the care of every houseplant in existence, the following chapter contains information about some of the most common and beloved houseplants, along with some that you may not be familiar with.

My intent is to provide you with specific care details, based on my experience, on a number of plants that may help you on your journey. Perhaps you'd like to solidify how to care for certain plants, and once you've mastered those, you'd like to expand your collection. When you feel comfortable growing some "easier" houseplants, don't be afraid to try something new!

I've chosen to group plants together by plant family. Plants that fall within the same family share certain characteristics that help us identify them. Plants in the same family may have some similarities, including the appearance of flowers, and these similarities can give us clues about how to grow them. It is also fun to know which plants are related to each other.

Plant Party

This section contains plants organized alphabetically by plant family. Within each plant family, the individual plant profiles are organized alphabetically by common name (and with the botanical name in parenthesis).

Hoya flower

APOCYNACEAE FAMILY OF PLANTS

The Apocynaceae family of plants, sometimes referred to as the dogbane or milkweed plant family, contains some wonderful houseplants. I've chosen to discuss the care of four different genera from this family: *Dischidia, Hoya, Huernia,* and *Ceropegia* (string of hearts).

True to the milkweed name, many of the plants in this family ooze out a sticky, white latex. If you've broken the stem of a *Dischidia,* you will know what I'm talking about! I live in a region where common milkweed (*Asclepias syriaca*), which is part of this same plant family, grows. This plant is a food source for monarch butterfly caterpillars, and if you have ever seen the flowers of a milkweed, then you know they are strikingly similar to those of *Hoyas!*

Huernia zebrina flower

LIFESAVER CACTUS
(*Huernia zebrina*)

Native to a few countries in southern Africa. Despite its common name, it is not a cactus but a succulent. This is a great plant for low humidity environments, and it tolerates neglect very well.

LIGHT: In nature, these plants are low-growing succulents and typically grow under shrubs. Indoors, you'll want enough sun to generate strong growth and flowering, but not so much sun that it scalds. My own plant grows happily directly in front of an eastern-facing window and benefits from morning sun. Avoid harsher midday sun. Western windows would also work. Whatever window you use, some direct sun is beneficial, but not all-day sun.

POTTING MIX: I use a blend that I use for most succulents, which is two parts succulent/cactus potting mix plus one part ¼-inch pumice.

WATERING: Allow at least the top inch of soil to dry out in between thorough watering. Most of the time, I let all the potting mix dry out, especially during wintertime.

PROPAGATION: It is very simple to propagate these plants. My own plant was grown from a 1-inch cutting that a friend sent me in the mail. When taking a small cutting, allow it to air-dry for a few days so the cut will callous over and dry, which will prevent rotting. Then simply insert the cutting into potting mix, water it, and wait. When the surface is completely dry, you can water again. My plant flowered for the first time about two years after propagating from a small cutting.

TIPS:

- Light that is too low will produce weak growth and no flowering. Too much sun will cause the plant to turn reddish or even purplish. If you see this, decrease the amount of direct sun a bit.
- These plants can be very top heavy, so I keep mine in a terra cotta pot. Terra cotta is a great choice for succulents since they need to dry out quickly in between watering.

MILLION HEARTS PLANT
(*Dischidia ruscifolia*)

Native to tropical and subtropical Asia and West Pacific, this epiphytic genus (meaning it grows on the surface of other plants, in this case trees) is still little-known, but I've found them to make delightful houseplants! There are over 100 species of *Dischidia*, and very few of them are being cultivated. I currently grow three species: *ruscifolia* (million hearts plant), *nummularia* (string of nickels), and *ovata* (watermelon dischidia). *Dischidia* is closely related to *Hoya*. If you are comfortable growing *Hoyas*, you might love this plant genus.

LIGHT: Mostly bright indirect light right in front of a window is the way to go with these plants. A couple of hours of direct sun in early morning or late afternoon is beneficial.

POTTING MIX: These are epiphytes and they grow best in a very chunky potting mix. I grow my *Dischidia nummularia* and *Dischidia ruscifolia* in pure coconut husk chunks. You can also use a medium grade orchid bark. When I received my *Dischidia*

ovata, it was growing in what appeared to be a plain all-purpose potting mix with some perlite added in. I continue to grow it in that medium given that it has been growing well.

WATERING: Allow the potting media to dry out almost completely, and then give them a good soaking. Because they are epiphytes and absorb water through their leaves as well, be sure to wet the leaves too.

PROPAGATION: You can easily root these plants with stem cuttings. Be careful when you make the cuttings. When cut, they will secrete a milky white fluid that can irritate your skin.

TIPS:

- These plants are well suited to growing in hanging baskets.
- When happy, *Dischidia ruscifolia* will produce very tiny, usually whitish, flowers that can be surprisingly fragrant.
- Don't be afraid to frequently mist these plants since they are epiphytes and are adapted to absorb moisture through their leaves.

STRING OF HEARTS
(*Ceopegia woodii* subsp. *woodii*)

Native to southern parts of Africa. This delightful vining plant will grow several feet long, will grow dainty flowers, and is easy to propagate.

LIGHT: For best growth, give your plant at least a few hours of direct sun. These are not low-light plants.

POTTING MIX: A very well-draining potting mix is crucial. I like to use about two parts of a cactus/succulent mix with one part pumice.

WATERING: Wait until the top half of the potting mix is dry before watering again.

PROPAGATION: This plant propagates readily from cuttings. Take stem cuttings and either root them in water or place them directly in potting mix. You can also lay the stem cuttings horizontally right on top of potting mix and they will root. Another option is to lay the tubers that form on the vines right on top of the potting mix and they will root.

TIPS:

- If you don't give your plant enough light, it will be apparent by larger internodes. In other words, the leaves will be spaced out more.
- Like most plants, avoid letting this one sit in water. On the other end, don't allow the potting mix to go completely dry for too long or it will result in many crispy brown leaves dropping off your plant.

WAX PLANT (*Hoya* spp.)

Native to tropical and subtropical Asia as well as the West Pacific, these epiphytes are a joy to grow and will reward you with fragrant flowers under the right conditions. *Hoyas* come in a wide array of leaf shapes and sizes, and you can easily form a collection just of this genus! Most *Hoya* species have very thick, succulent leaves, making most of them suited to tolerate neglect as well as low humidity.

LIGHT: Although *Hoya* are tolerant of lower light, they do best right in front of a window. Give them with a few hours of direct sun if you can, but not all-day sun.

POTTING MIX: I like to use two parts cactus/succulent mix plus one part ¼-inch pumice. This mix provides great drainage.

WATERING: Allow your *Hoyas* to dry out almost completely before watering thoroughly again. These are great plants for busy people because they tolerate dry conditions and neglect very well.

PROPAGATION: *Hoyas* can be propagated by stem cuttings, which can be either rooted in water or directly in a moist potting mix.

TIPS:

- To encourage blooming, try and keep your *Hoyas* root-bound and give your plants a dry period of a month or so in the winter. Cooler temperatures in the winter will also help.

- *Hoyas* can stay in the same pot for quite a few years. Don't rush to repot. My large *Hoya carnosa* has been in the same pot that I purchased it in, and I've had it for over 15 years.

- *Never* prune your *Hoyas* unless the vines are dead. Also, do not ever remove the flowering spurs. Once flowering occurs and the petals fall off, leave the spurs because they will rebloom in that same location.

- There are so many species to grow. Here are some of my favorites, but there are many more that you might wish to explore!

  - *Hoya carnosa:* This is maybe the most commonly available *Hoya*. Some varieties are plain green and others are variegated. The flowers are large and fragrant.

  - *Hoya carnosa 'Compacta':* This is the Hindu rope plant, and it features crinkled leaves. Keep an eye out for mealybugs because all the nooks and crannies make plenty of hiding places for pests.

  - *Hoya curtisii:* This plant has small, heart-shaped leaves with beautiful gray mottling.

- *Hoya multiflora:* Commonly called the shooting star hoya because of the flowers' appearance, this is a particularly free-blooming species. The leaves are not nearly as succulent as many other *Hoya* species, so be careful not to leave this one dry for too long.
- *Hoya linearis:* This higher altitude *Hoya* has skinny, soft, and slightly hairy leaves, unlike many *Hoya* species. It has a lovely growing habit and prefers cooler temperatures than most *Hoyas*.
- *Hoya obovata:* This one has stunning foliage with very succulent, oval leaves that often have splashes of white or pink markings.

Hoya carnosa

ARACEAE FAMILY OF PLANTS (AROIDS)

So many of the popular plants that are grown indoors belong to the Araceae plant family, or Aroid plant family. These include *Aglaonema* (Chinese evergreen), *Alocasia, Anthurium, Monstera, Philodendron, Epipremnum* (pothos), *Rhaphidophora, Spathiphyllum* (peace lily), and *Zamioculcas zamiifolia* (ZZ plant), all of which I discuss in this section. There are many more, of course!

Monstera deliciosa

Peace lily inflorescence

One easy way to identify an Aroid is by looking at their inflorescence, or flowering structure. Aroid inflorescences have a central structure called a spadix, in which there are many tiny flowers. The spathe is the leaflike structure behind the spadix. Plants in the Araceae family all have similar flowering structures.

Unless otherwise noted, for all the Aroids in this section, I use the same potting mix in most cases, which is three parts all-purpose potting mix with one part of perlite. You can adjust as needed, of course, to suit your conditions.

CHINESE EVERGREEN
(*Aglaonema* spp.)

An Asian tropical forest native, spanning from India to Papua New Guinea. These plants come in a stunning array of colors from green to pinks and reds. Chinese evergreens are among the best foliage plants for the indoor environment, tolerating low humidity and lower light than most plants.

LIGHT: These plants are among those you can grow in your home that can tolerate lower light. Green varieties can grow in pretty dim light, often even far away from a window. If your light is too dark, the foliage on the more brightly colored *Aglaonema* will fade. These will all grow nicely in front of eastern or western windows, or even in front of any window with no direct sun at all.

WATERING: Allow the top quarter of the pot to dry out before watering thoroughly again.

PROPAGATION: *Aglaonema* can easily be propagated by either division at the roots or by stem cuttings. Simply cut one of the canes and place it in water to root. When the roots are about an inch long, plant in potting mix.

TIPS:

- Although these grow in humid jungles, they are pretty tolerant of average indoor humidity.
- Occasionally these will flower. No one grows these plants for their flowers, so it is best to cut them off so that the plants can focus more on leaf growth.

Aglaonema 'Cutlass'

An *Alocasia* I've had for numerous years that I bring outdoors every summer.

ELEPHANT EARS
(*Alocasia* spp.)

Species in the *Alocasia* genus are native to tropical and subtropical Asia as well as eastern Australia. There are various species and hybrids available, but all exhibit the same finicky disposition. This plant is one of the most challenging plants to grow well indoors, so don't feel bad if yours is not thriving! Our indoor environment is not hospitable for certain plants, and *Alocasia* is among them. These plants do best with consistently warm, humid conditions, which are difficult to provide in the average home.

LIGHT: Place your *Alocasia* right in front of a window that receives about a couple of hours of direct sun. Avoid locations with too much direct sun, but by all means keep it very close to a window.

WATERING: Aim to keep your plant pretty consistently moist. Allow the top inch to dry out and then water.

PROPAGATION: Plants will produce off-shoots at the base, which you can divide.

TIPS:

- Some plants just aren't the easiest houseplants. This is definitely one of them, but it is possible to grow them. Just don't expect them to look like they did the day you brought them home from a nursery. Besides the appropriate light, the challenging part is that they need consistently warm and humid conditions as well as consistently damp potting mix.
- If conditions are not ideal, your plant will go dormant. Potting mixes that are too dry, as well as temperatures that are too cold, can cause your plant to stall and induce dormancy.
- Try and find an appropriately warm room with good light and increase humidity for best results. When all else fails, move the plant outdoors into complete shade during warm weather. It will reward you with wonderful growth.
- This plant is very prone to spider mites, so keep an eye out for them and treat them accordingly (see Key 6, page 89, for advice on controlling these pests).

FLAMINGO FLOWER
(*Anthurium* spp.)

Native to tropical forest habitat in Mexico, Central America, and South America. Typically, this plant is an epiphyte (it grows on other plants, in this case trees) or climbing hemiepiphyte (it spends only part of its lifecycle as an epiphyte), but it is also found as a terrestrial grower. A happy plant will be in constant bloom!

LIGHT: These plants like mostly bright, indirect light, but a couple of hours of direct sun in the home can also be beneficial. Placing your plants directly in front of an eastern window works beautifully. Avoid midday sun, which is typically too strong for these plants.

POTTING MIX: I've had great success with the following mix: one part all-purpose potting mix with one part perlite and one part orchid bark.

WATERING: A balance is needed with watering this plant for best results. Allow your potting media to dry out about a quarter of the way down, and then soak your plant. Do not allow your potting mix to dry out completely, especially for longer periods, or you will see numerous yellow leaves.

PROPAGATION: This can be done either by division at the roots or by cuttings. You will find that this plant typically extends over time, and you will often see aerial roots forming.

TIPS:

- If your plant is not flowering, increase the light levels a bit, and fertilize if you haven't been fertilizing.
- These plants love warm conditions and high humidity. It is helpful to run a humidifier to increase humidity.
- The inflorescences are waxy and long-lasting, and they commonly come in red, white, and even pink.
- With time, the plant will grow and need a support. My own plant is well over 15 years old, is almost 2 feet tall, and is supported by a small trellis. As the plant gets larger with age, it can be continually in bloom year-round. My own plant has literally been in continual bloom for years.
- There are many other species of *Anthurium* that are grown for their stunning foliage (such as *Anthurium clarinervium*). If you are more of a beginning houseplant enthusiast, you may want to try gaining confidence with the much more common flamingo flower before venturing into growing the other, more expensive and harder to find *Anthurium* species.

RIGHT: My red-flowered *Anthurium*.

HEART LEAF PHILODENDRON AND 'BRASIL' CULTIVAR
(*Philodendron hederaceum*)

This vine is native to Mexico and Central and South America. The classic, plain green heart leaf philodendron has been a houseplant standard for so many years, and it's one that I still cherish! The 'Brasil' cultivar puts a twist on the classic plant with its green and yellow variegated leaves.

LIGHT: These are wonderful plants for windows that receive no direct sun. That being said, they can take a little direct sun, especially in the wintertime, when light is normally at a premium. The 'Brasil' cultivar needs a little more light than the plain green version.

WATERING: These are pretty tough plants and tolerate a variety of conditions. For optimal health, allow no more than about the top quarter of the potting mix to dry out before watering thoroughly again.

PROPAGATION: These are very simple to propagate. Simply take small stem cuttings and place them in water or directly in a moist potting mix. They will root easily. Often, you will see aerial roots already present at the nodes on the vine.

Heart leaf philodendron

TIPS:

- This is one plant that I'm comfortable with in dimmer conditions and even a few feet away from a window. Just temper your expectations if you do place it in lower light. This plant is quite a vigorous grower, especially the plain green heart leaf philodendron. If your plant is not growing much, move it to a brighter location.
- Given that they are enthusiastic growers, don't be afraid to prune the plants back a bit. I regularly have to trim mine to keep them inbounds. Pruning also helps keep the plants vigorous.

MINI MONSTERA
(*Rhaphidophora tetrasperma*)

This native of Thailand and Malaysia is becoming more and more popular and widespread, and for good reason! Under good care, it grows very quickly and is a cinch to propagate. It is sometimes called mini monstera because the leaves look similar to *Monstera deliciosa*, but it does not belong to the *Monstera* genus.

LIGHT: Keep these plants near a window for best growth, in a location that gets mostly indirect light. A couple of hours of direct sun in early morning or late afternoon is beneficial for growth indoors.

WATERING: In my experience, these plants grow best when I keep the potting mix pretty evenly moist. I try and wait for just the surface of the mix to dry out, and then I water again.

PROPAGATION: These plants root very readily. Simply cut right below a node (where the leaf and petiole meet the stem). Root either in water or directly in a moist potting mix.

TIPS:

- These plants will grow rapidly, and often you need only one cutting to provide an endless supply of future material for propagation. They will grow several feet tall. If you want a full plant versus just a single stemmed plant, take several cuttings, root them, and plant them all in the same pot.

- These plants will need some kind of support as they grow. Use a single long stake for support and tie them to the support. If you have multiple stems in the same pot, you can make a bamboo tripod. Insert three bamboo stakes into the pot and tie them on top.

PEACE LILY
(*Spathiphyllum* spp.)

Spathiphyllum species are native to Mexico, tropical America, and also Malaysia and West Pacific regions. They are typically found in humid tropical forest floors. Although they have stringent requirements for soil moisture, they are among the best plants for lower-light areas and easily tolerate the average home environment.

LIGHT: These plants flourish in front of windows that have bright indirect light. If there is any direct sun, keep it to a minimum of one to two hours at the most in the early morning or late afternoon sun. They are also one of the best plants to "push the limit" in terms of low-light conditions. I often have them placed throughout the house where other plants won't grow so I can use valuable window real estate for other plants.

WATERING: Although you should never let this plant sit in water for any period of time, aim to keep the potting mix moist. If you water as soon as the surface of the mix feels dry, your plant will thank you. Never allow the potting mix to become completely dry.

PROPAGATION: Propagate by division. Simply take your plant out of the pot and divide it up at the roots into as many plants as you want.

TIPS:

- These broad-leaved plants will readily collect dust, so be sure to periodically rinse off the leaves or gently wipe each leaf with a moist sponge. You may also notice white, dusty material on the plant leaves. If your plant is flowering, this is simply pollen that has fallen on the leaves.

- If your plant is not flowering, move it to brighter light. Even in dim conditions where I keep my various peace lilies, they still flower, although meagerly. If you want a bigger show, increase light levels and fertilize during the growing season.

- A common issue often seen with this plant is total drooping and wilting of the entire plant. If you see this, go ahead and *feel your potting mix immediately.* Wilting of the entire plant is most often due to your potting mix having gone completely dry, or the opposite case, where it has stayed wet for so long that the plant has developed root rot. If your plant has gone bone dry, take it to the sink or bathtub and soak it completely. Your plant will normally recover in a few hours. If it has stayed too wet, figure out why and take appropriate action (see the root rot section in Key 6, page 85). Was it sitting in water? Is it in a pot without a drainage hole? Avoid letting your plant get to the wilting state repeatedly. Repeated wilting will damage your plant to the point of no return.

- Brown tips are common with this plant, especially if you don't keep the potting mix fairly evenly moist. Simply cut the brown tips off and be sure to pay more attention to your watering routine.

A blooming peace lily.

- *Spathiphyllum* can be sensitive to built-up salts in their potting mix from fertilizers or tap water. If you see any crusty residue on the surface of the potting mix and there are excessive brown edges on the leaves, despite otherwise good care, you may want to repot your plant into fresh potting mix and give your plant a good flush with plain water to help remove any built-up salts.

- Yellow leaves often happen quite readily with potting mix that is kept too dry.

PHILODENDRON 'PINK PRINCESS'
(Philodendron erubescens)

Philodendron erubescens is native to Colombia. 'Pink Princess' is a wildly popular philodendron with very dark, almost black leaves and hot pink variegation. No two plants are exactly alike.

LIGHT: Light is an important factor in helping to maximize the beautiful coloration in this plant. Set these plants right in front of a window with plenty of bright indirect light. At a minimum, a couple of hours of direct sun in the early morning or late afternoon is helpful.

WATERING: Let the soil dry down a bit, up to about the top quarter of the potting mix, before watering again.

PROPAGATION: You can easily propagate these with stem cuttings. Cut right under a node (where the leaf and petiole meet the vine itself) and root in water or directly in a moist potting mix. Aerial roots are normally visible, so the process should be quite simple.

TIPS:

- These are climbers, so you will need to provide some kind of support as they grow. A moss post or bamboo stake will do.
- Everyone seems to want completely pink leaves, and they do appear! However, the plant cannot support them for long because there is no chlorophyll in those leaves. Enjoy them while they last.
- As your plant grows, you may see all pink leaves, or your plant could even revert to solid green leaves. If you see this, then you'll want to rebalance the leaf coloration. Start at the top of the vine and work your way down until you find the first leaf that exhibits a more balanced variegation. Cut the vine right above this leaf. The resulting growth should exhibit more balanced coloration.

POTHOS OR DEVIL'S IVY
(*Epipremnum aureum*)

Native to French Polynesia. Pothos are often one of the first plants that budding houseplant enthusiasts will grow, and rightfully so. These vines are tolerant of a wide variety of conditions, grow rapidly, and are a cinch to propagate. They are one of the best plants to grow in lower light and require no special attention to humidity.

LIGHT: Pothos are remarkably versatile houseplants that tolerate a wide range in light. I've grown tremendous pothos specimens in windowless offices, but those locations had overhead fluorescent lighting on all day. Few plants will grow as well in such conditions. Better growth will occur, though, in front of a window, and pothos can easily handle up to about half a day of direct sun. Note that if the position is too sunny, all the leaves will turn a yellowish-green. That is your indication to reduce the amount of light if you don't like the appearance.

WATERING: Wait until the surface of the potting mix is dry before watering again. I try not to let more than the top quarter of the potting mix dry out.

PROPAGATION: Pothos propagate readily by cuttings. You can use single node cuttings, or you can make cuttings of portions of the vine that are a few inches long each. Don't make them too long, otherwise your cuttings will struggle. Propagate in water or directly in moist potting mix.

TIPS:

- Pothos like it warm. If you have any chilly or drafty locations, they may struggle there.
- These vines are traditionally sold as hanging plants, but you can also grow them supported by a moss post or any other support structure. The roots will attach to the supporting structure and start climbing. Outdoors in warm climates, you will see them growing up tree trunks, but they also grow as a groundcover.
- If you are propagating this plant and you want a pot that is nice and full of foliage, don't just add one or two cuttings to a pot and hope that it will grow full and bushy. It won't happen. Add several cuttings to the pot.
- There are many stunning pothos cultivars available. Keep in mind that the more heavily variegated ones will have a slower growth rate. Here are just some of the most popular pothos cultivars:
  - 'Marble Queen' is a heavily variegated plant with a lot of white in the foliage.
  - 'Snow Queen' is similar to 'Marble Queen' but the variegation in 'Snow Queen' is more consistent, and there is more white variegation.
  - 'Neon' pothos is a shocking chartreuse color.
  - 'Manjula,' which has cream, white, and green as well as some silver and yellowish green variegated foliage.
  - 'N' Joy' and 'Pearls and Jade' have smaller leaves than most pothos

Golden pothos is one of the best plants to grow in locations that are not right in front of a window.

and look very similar to each other with beautiful green leaves that have whitish to yellowish variegation. 'Pearls and Jade' can be distinguished from 'N' Joy' because of the addition of tiny splashes of green in the leaves.

- 'Cebu Blue' is actually a different species (*Epipremnum pinnatum*) but is still considered a pothos. Juvenile leaves have a gorgeous silvery-green color and narrower leaves than other types of pothos. These grow pretty vigorously.

SWISS CHEESE PLANT
(*Monstera deliciosa*)

Native to southern Mexico and Central America, this plant is a beast and can grow extremely large, even in a home setting. Despite its exotic looks (it's popular for its big, unique leaves), it is very tolerant of average indoors conditions and makes for a wonderful houseplant. Nothing beats the large fenestrations on mature plants. Make sure you have a lot of room, because this plant will get quite sizeable over the years!

LIGHT: Similar to most *Monsteras*, these plants grow best in front of a window that has plenty of bright indirect light, but even a couple of hours of direct sun in the morning or late afternoon works wonderfully. They can grow in more direct sun, but you may find that the entire plant will turn a yellowish-green. My own plant grows in front of a large wall of eastern-facing windows.

WATERING: Allow your potting mix to dry at least an inch or so on the surface, and up to the top half of the potting mix, before watering thoroughly again. Don't let it get completely dry to the point where the plant is drooping.

PROPAGATION: You can easily propagate by cuttings. Be sure to include one or two leaves, and cut on either side of the vine where the leaf and petiole meet the vine. Or, if you just want one cutting, simply cut the tip of the vine right below a node. You will often already see an aerial root on the vine at this location. Place in water to root or plant directly into a small pot with a moist potting mix. Keep humidity high if you can while the cutting is rooting, as it is becoming established.

TIPS:

- These are climbing plants, and you will eventually need to provide some kind of support. I personally use three bamboo posts that I tie on top to make a tripod structure. As the plant grows, I simply tie them to the structure. You can also use a moss post if you'd like.
- As your plant gets larger, it is handy to place it on a sturdy caster with wheels. This way you can easily move the plant as needed and also easily rotate the plant so it grows more evenly.
- Don't be shocked when your plant starts to grow aerial roots. You can direct them into the pot so they can start growing into the potting mix. My own plant is growing so many that they're cascading over the pot and onto the floor.
- Juvenile leaves will have no fenestrations in the foliage. As the plant gets older, the new foliage will progressively have more holes and slits. This comes with time, so you'll have to exercise patience if you have a young plant!

SWISS CHEESE VINE
(*Monstera adansonii*)

Native to southern Mexico through much of South America. This extremely vigorous grower has numerous holes, or fenestrations, hence the common name.

LIGHT: These plants are adaptable to a variety of light conditions. In nature, they often start growing on the forest floor and climb up a tree where they may end up near a canopy that has brighter light. Bright indirect or filtered light very close to a window will suit these plants well, but they will also be fine with two to three hours of morning or late afternoon sun.

WATERING: Allow at least the top inch or so of the potting mix, up to maybe the top quarter, to dry out before watering again. Avoid extreme dryness or you will quickly get multiple yellow leaves.

PROPAGATION: Propagation is super simple with stem cuttings that are a few inches long. Pot them up directly into a moist potting mix, or start to root them in water and then transfer to potting mix. Aerial roots are almost always visible at the nodes (where the leaf and petiole meet the vine). If you utilize single node cuttings and place several in a pot, each one will grow a vine and it will result in a fuller plant.

TIPS:

- Often sold as hanging baskets, you can also train these plants to grow up a moss pole, rough slab of wood, or support stakes.
- This plant is probably the fastest growing houseplant I own. I started out with just three or four cuttings from a friend. As it grew, I continually took cuttings and planted them back in the original pot. With persistence, you can easily get a nice, full specimen this way.
- Juvenile plants have leaves with no fenestrations. As the plant grows over time, it will have more fenestrations, especially if given a climbing support to attach onto.
- If you want to explore growing other *Monstera* species, there are quite a few you can try once you get comfortable with their care. I've found that *Monstera siltepecana* likes the same conditions as *adansonii* and has a similar growth habit, but has beautiful dark green veins and grey-ish green leaves in its juvenile form.

ZZ PLANT
(*Zamioculcas zamiifolia*)

Native to several countries in Eastern Africa, this Aroid is tough as nails and can survive quite a bit of neglect. This is one of the best beginner plants, period. Tolerant of dry soil, low light, and low humidity, this is a great plant to build confidence with.

LIGHT: The ZZ plant is very versatile when it comes to light conditions. It can survive very dim conditions, but it will have better growth with brighter light. Any window exposure will suffice, but I would probably avoid direct sun all day.

POTTING MIX: I like to mix two parts cactus/succulent mix with one part perlite or pumice.

WATERING: ZZ plant will tolerate great amounts of neglect when it comes to watering. I allow all my potting mix to dry out completely before watering thoroughly. It can stay dry for quite a long time, so this is a great plant for the forgetful waterer!

PROPAGATION: Propagation by division at the roots is the quickest way to make more plants. You can also propagate from individual leaves and either place them in water or directly into a 50/50 potting mix and perlite blend. It's fun to watch a rhizome form right at the base of the leaf. If you choose water propagation, make sure that you don't keep the leaves in water for too long, otherwise the leaves can rot. With patient and persistent care, you should see new shoots form after a few months. You can also propagate by cutting off a whole stalk and placing it in water or soil mix. See page 111 for illustrated examples of ZZ plant leaf propagation.

TIPS:

- If you've had your plant for more than a year and it hasn't grown much at all, you may want to consider increasing light. These plants can survive for a long time even far away from a window, but their growth may be disappointing in these locations.
- Propagation can take a very long time. To increase the speed, keep your cuttings warm by using a seedling heating mat.
- This plant seems to be very pest-tolerant. I have yet to see a pest on my ZZ plant!
- ZZ 'Raven' is a stunning cultivar and offers a twist on the plain green ZZ plant. The new leaves on 'Raven' emerge a lovely bright green and mature to a deep purple, almost black, leaf.

ASPARAGACEAE FAMILY OF PLANTS

As you can deduce from the name, the Asparagaceae plant family is commonly referred to as the Asparagus plant family. I've included two wonderful plants from this family: *Beaucarnea recurvata* (Ponytail Palm) and Snake Plants (formerly the *Sansevieria* genus, and reclassified into the *Dracaena* genus).

PONYTAIL PALM
(*Beaucarnea recurvata*)

Native to Mexico. These sturdy plants form a big caudex (swollen base) with a fountain of foliage emerging from it. Although they are commonly called Ponytail Palms, they are not palms at all, but rather, succulent. These are perfect plants for bright areas with low humidity and are great plants for the neglectful indoor gardener.

LIGHT: Give your Ponytail Palm at least half a day of direct sun, if not more, for best growth. My own plant sits right in front of a large Eastern facing window and does beautifully. These are not low light plants. If you place your plant in low light, they will often survive and look acceptable for a while, but they will eventually weaken and decline over time.

POTTING MIX: I use my standard succulent mix, which is two parts cactus/succulent mix with one part ¼-inch pumice added in.

WATERING: These plants need to dry out a bit in between watering. Allow the top half of the potting mix to dry out before watering again.

PROPAGATION: If your plant has any offsets or pups, cut it away from the mother plant and pot it up. If you're not comfortable with propagation, you may want to not even attempt it. Unless you want a single-trunk specimen, there is nothing wrong with leaving multiple plants in one pot.

TIPS:

- Although you should allow at least your top half of the potting mix to dry out, try to avoid allowing it to stay bone dry for too long. The plant's bottom leaves will naturally turn brown, but drought conditions will accelerate this and cause a lot of the lower leaves to turn brown. When leaves have turned completely brown, grasp each leaf and gently pull it off the plant.
- Expect brown tips on your plant. There is no avoiding it. Even plants in nature have brown tips, so you should delight in this fact and not expect perfection! I simply cut the brown tips off occasionally with scissors.
- Resist the urge to overpot this plant. Only go up one pot size when you do repot so that your potting mix still dries out in a reasonable amount of time. They can stay in the same pot for quite a few years before needing to be repotted again.

Various snake plants

SNAKE PLANT
(*Dracaena trifasciata*)

Commonly known as Snake Plant or Mother in Law's Tongue, this African-native genus *Sansevieria* has recently been reclassified into the *Dracaena* genus. They come in many shapes, sizes, and growth habits. Snake Plants are among the most indestructible, unfussy houseplants that are very robust to neglect and don't give a hoot about low humidity!

LIGHT: These plants are remarkably versatile when it comes to light. These are often classified as "low light" plants, but don't be fooled. Although they can tolerate low light, they will slowly decline, weaken, and slow in growth. I have witnessed these plants growing in their native Africa, and in other warm climates, in full sun. Although they don't need full sun in the home, they will benefit from some direct sun for sturdier and faster growth. You can place them in front of virtually any window exposure and they will grow.

POTTING MIX: I personally use two parts of a cactus/succulent potting mix plus one part ¼-inch pumice. They need very well-draining potting mixes that dry out fairly quickly.

WATERING: Allow your plants to dry out completely and then water thoroughly. Do not allow your plant to sit in water, as they can easily rot this way.

PROPAGATION: The simplest and fastest way to propagate is simply by division. Divide a plant that has multiple crowns, and pot up each portion in a separate pot. You can also propagate with leaf cuttings. See the propagation chapter for a detailed overview.

TIPS:

- Be careful of getting water in the crown of your plant, as this can encourage rotting. Blow it out or use a sponge or towel to absorb any standing water.
- Occasionally they will flower indoors, and the flowers are fragrant.
- Although these plants can survive for long periods in dim corners, you will get much better growth by keeping these plants in brighter light.
- There are many different species and cultivars available, and you can easily start a collection. *Dracaena trifasciata* is the plain version that can grow 3 or 4 feet tall. 'Laurentii' is a cultivar with beautiful yellow edges on the leaves. *Dracaena masoniana*, commonly known as whale fin, has enormous leaves and you may only get one new leaf per year. 'Hahnii' only grows a few inches tall, but it will spread into a lovely clump over many years. 'Bantel's Sensation' is a stunning narrow-leaved cultivar that has vertically striped green and white markings on its leaves.

BROMELIACEAE FAMILY OF PLANTS (BROMELIADS)

I've always been fascinated by the bromeliad plant family. Many members of the bromeliad plant family are epiphytic, meaning they grow on other plants, such as on tree limbs, versus growing in soil. These include *Aechmea fasciata* (urn plant) and the *Tillandsia* genus (air plants), both of which I discuss in this section.

Did you know that pineapples are also in the bromeliad plant family? Pineapples are a sun-loving bromeliad that are terrestrial and grow in soil versus epiphytically like many other bromeliads.

AIR PLANTS (*Tillandsia* spp.)

Native to much of Mexico and Central America and South America. Contrary to popular belief, air plants cannot survive on air alone. They need special attention paid to light and water for long-term growth. These tend to be much easier to grow if you can provide higher humidity.

LIGHT: Tillandsia species need to be in front of a window, and they relish filtered or bright indirect light. Be careful of giving them too much sun, but they will benefit from a couple of hours of morning sun or late afternoon sun, especially *Tillandsia xerographica*, which is healthiest when grown in at least a couple of hours, if not more, of direct sun.

POTTING MIX: None! They are normally kept loose or mounted on various objects. In nature, the roots are typically just a means to attach themselves onto tree branches, which is where they typically grow.

WATERING: These plants absorb moisture and nutrients through modified scales or hairs on their leaves called trichomes. You can water them by misting, running them under a faucet, dunking them in a bowl of water, or soaking them for a more extended period. With the exception of xeric types, such as *Tillandsia xerographica*, which grow in arid regions, most air plants require more attention to watering than most people realize. If you mist them even daily, it's sometimes not enough because some water will evaporate and not provide a deep enough watering. I prefer to soak them because it provides a deeper watering, and the plants can go longer in between watering. This is also the only good method to restore tillandsias that have become very dry. Soaking tillandsia once a week for an hour or two is a good way to keep them in good health. *Tillandsia xerographica* can often go for weeks without water. The leaves will get curlier when dry and they straighten out after a good soaking. Some people prefer to mist xeric types like the *tectorum* and *xerographica* species. Be sure to shake free any excess water to avoid rotting.

Tillandsia xerographica

PROPAGATION: After tillandias bloom, they will create pups or offsets at their base. You can leave them attached and they will grow into a clump, or if you want an individual specimen, you can carefully detach them when they're at least one-third the size of the parent plant. After the parent plant blooms and creates pups, it will start a very slow process of dying, which can take several months if not years.

TIPS:

- Tillandsias are epiphytes, so in nature they typically grow on tree branches. They use their roots solely to attach to their host plant, but they are not parasitic and don't derive any sustenance from their host trees. You may or may not have any roots on your indoor air plants, and it doesn't matter either way.

- There are two main types of plants in the genus *Tillandsia*. The first is the mesic type. *Mesic* comes from the Greek word for "middle," which speaks to areas with moderate amounts of moisture such as tropical forests. Mesic types tend to be greener and smoother due to less and smaller trichomes. They will require more frequent watering. Xeric types come from more arid climates with less humidity and rainfall. *Xeric* comes from the Greek word "dry," and these air plants often have larger and more trichomes and have a gray or silvery appearance. Xeric types like the *xerographica* species are pretty drought-tolerant and need much less frequent watering than mesic types.

- Make sure that water does not accumulate in your tillandsia plants for extended periods. Indoors, we don't have the benefit of air circulation, so you must turn your plants upside down and gently shake any excess water out in order to avoid rotting. You can even set them upside down on a towel to drip dry before returning them to their growing spot. If you have been soaking your air plants and shaking them free of excess water and they still rotted, then they may not have had sufficient light. If you keep your air plant in a dim location, over time it will decline, and sometimes soaking it will be the last straw.

- PRO TIP: Don't ignore fertilizing if you want to keep your tillandsias over the long term. Often, they will lose their vigor after a couple of years if you don't fertilize. There are fertilizers made specifically for bromeliads.

A *Tillandsia xerographica* soaking in a bowl of water.

URN PLANT
(Aechmea fasciata)

Native to the jungles of Brazil, these epiphytic bromeliads typically grow attached to trees, and they like it warm and humid. What most people would call the flower is actually the pink flower bract. The flowers themselves grow out of the pink bract and are much smaller.

LIGHT: These plants benefit from some direct sun, so place them right in front of an eastern or western window.

POTTING MIX: A good potting mix for these includes about two parts all-purpose potting mix, one part perlite, and one part orchid bark. You can also use one part all-purpose potting mix with one part perlite. These mixes provide a sharply draining and airy medium that bromeliads love.

WATERING: Allow your potting mix to dry out almost completely, and then soak it thoroughly. Always keep water in the central cup (where the flower bract emerges) right in the middle of the plant.

PROPAGATION: After these plants flower, they will grow offsets or pups at the base of the plant. These can be removed when the pups are about half the size of the mother plant, or you can just keep them growing in the same pot.

TIPS:

- Always keep the central cup filled with water.
- Keep in mind that after the mother plant flowers, it will start a slow process of dying, but the plant should produce pups. At the time of writing

The flower bract on an *Aechmea fasciata*.

this book, I'm on my third generation of pups!

- Under good conditions, if you grow your plant from pups to adulthood, these plants should bloom in approximately three to four years. If you're tired of waiting, once the plant is large enough, you can force your plant to bloom by placing it in a clear plastic bag with a couple of apples for two weeks. The apples emit ethylene gas, which will trigger blooming.

- Bromeliads have small root systems, so do *not* be tempted to grow these in large pots. In fact, I grow mine in 5-inch terra cotta pots and they do beautifully. It is helpful to grow these in heavier pots (terra cotta, ceramic, and so forth) because they can be quite top-heavy.

CACTACEAE FAMILY OF PLANTS (CACTUS)

When we think of any plants in the cactus family, the first thing that comes to mind is probably a prickly desert cactus. My favorite cacti to grow are actually jungle cacti, and in this section, I talk about the care of three genera: *Epiphyllum, Rhipsalis,* and *Schlumbergera.* These plants are very different from their desert cousins in that they grow in humid jungles and are epiphytes, meaning that they grow on other plants, typically trees.

They make delightful houseplants, and you may already be familiar with growing Thanksgiving cactus, Christmas cactus, and some others.

Epiphyllum oxypetalum flower

CHRISTMAS AND THANKSGIVING CACTUS (*Schlumbergera* spp.)

Native to Brazil, these jungle cacti are very long-lived and are often passed down as heirloom plants. Thanksgiving cacti have points on their leaf segments, whereas Christmas cactus leaf segments are rounder, but the care is identical.

LIGHT: In order for flowering and good growth to occur, these plants must have enough light, so give them plenty of light right in front of a window. Eastern-exposure or western-exposure windows are ideal in most cases. They do not want to be in sun all day though, and you can tell if they are getting too much sun if they turn purple.

POTTING MIX: A standard mix of three parts all-purpose potting mix with one part perlite works well.

WATERING: Allow the potting mix to dry out somewhat in between watering. Wait until the top half of the mix has dried out, and then water thoroughly. Don't allow the potting mix to dry out completely, especially while the plant is in bud or flowering, otherwise you may experience bud drop.

PROPAGATION: Simply take cuttings of the leaf segments, allow them to dry for a couple of days to callous over, and then plant them in a moist potting mix.

- If you have your plant in a good location with sufficient light, but it is not blooming, it could be that it doesn't have uninterrupted darkness during the evening hours. Even if you turn on a light for a short period of time at night, this can be enough to prevent the plant from flowering. If your plant is in a location where you typically have lights on, move your plant to another location that would provide uninterrupted darkness during evening hours. Having a location that has cooler night temperatures is also beneficial for flowering.

- Bud drop is common if your potting mix is too dry or too wet. Pay special attention to your plant during the flowering period so you can enjoy the show.

- Be sure to regularly rotate your plant so that the entire plant will set flower, and not just the side facing the window.

- I once grew a Christmas cactus in front of a very large northern-exposure sliding door for over a decade, and it bloomed for four to five months every year because of its sheer size. These plants only get better with age.

A blooming Thanksgiving cactus.

MISTLETOE CACTUS
(*Rhipsalis* spp.)

This jungle cactus genus has species native to much of tropical and subtropical America, Africa, and also West Indian Ocean locations and Sri Lanka.

LIGHT: These plants grow as epiphytes attached to trees in nature, so they mainly will get filtered light. In the home environment, be sure to situate these plants right in front of a window with plenty of bright, indirect light. A couple of hours of direct sun is beneficial, especially during the wintertime when they can take quite a bit of sun. If you are disappointed in the growth, increase the light your plant receives.

Two of my *Rhipsalis* plants.

POTTING MIX: As epiphytes, *Rhipsalis* require a sharply draining mix and one that dries out pretty quickly. You can experiment with different mixes, but I've been successful growing these in two parts cactus/succulent mix with one part ¼-inch pumice. You can also try equal parts all-purpose potting mix, perlite, and orchid bark.

WATERING: Allow the potting medium to mostly dry out and then soak thoroughly. Be sure to also wet the leaves since epiphytes benefit from this.

PROPAGATION: Take cuttings, let them dry out and callous over for a couple of days, and then simply insert them into a moist potting mix. Keep the mix fairly moist, but allow the surface to dry before watering again. They root very readily.

TIPS:

- *Rhipsalis* have a pendulous growing nature, so these are best grown in a hanging basket.
- Avoid placing these in large pots. Keep their quarters pretty tight, and the rule of thumb of going up only one pot size when pot-bound really applies to these plants. In nature they go through many wet-dry cycles, so they need to dry out quickly in between watering.
- There are so many delightful species to try, including:
  - *Rhipsalis campos-portoana* has a mass of slender and smooth stems.
  - *Rhipsalis baccifera* has smooth and much thicker stems than *campos-portoana*.
  - *Rhipsalis paradoxa* has unusual, long, angled stems that can hang down a few feet.
  - *Rhipsalis pilocarpa* has hairy stems.

Epiphyllum oxypetalum flowers opening at night.

QUEEN OF THE NIGHT
(*Epiphyllum oxypetalum*)

Native to southern Mexico and Central America, this jungle cactus is notorious for its stunning, enormous flowers that open for one night only and close by dawn. It's worth the wait for the spectacular show!

LIGHT: These plants are epiphytes that typically grow in filtered light in nature. Situate these plants right in front of a window with mostly bright, indirect light. Two to three hours of sun is beneficial, especially to ensure that flowering occurs indoors.

POTTING MIX: I grow my own plant in equal parts all-purpose potting mix, perlite, and orchid bark. This provides the very sharp drainage that these epiphytes love.

WATERING: Allow the top quarter of the potting mix to dry out before thoroughly watering again.

PROPAGATION: Take 4- to 6-inch cuttings of the leaves (which are actually modified stems). Let them dry and callous over, and then insert them into a moist potting mix to root.

TIPS:

- These plants can get extremely large, so make sure you have the room. Sometimes they are sold in hanging planters, but they can get very awkward over time. I find that they're best grown as floor plants, because they will eventually get several feet tall. When your plant gets this size, it will require a support.
- In periods of the year with lower light, you may find that your plant will grow long, leafless growths. These are called stolons. In nature, these plants will grow stolons in order to search for higher light. Once they have enough light, the stolons will leaf out and start to grow. You can always prune these off if they get too awkward indoors.
- The fragrant flowers will typically appear in spring or summer and only last one night, so keep an eye out for them. The bud will grow several inches long before it opens at dusk. They will be closed by dawn the next day.

CRASSULACEAE FAMILY OF PLANTS

The Crassulaceae plant family, commonly called the stonecrop plant family, contains some very popular succulent houseplants including echeveria and jade plants, both of which are discussed in this section. Some other well-known houseplants in this family also include *Kalanchoe,* and the popular and hardy *Sempervivum* (hens and chicks).

HENS AND CHICKS
(*Echeveria* 'Hercules')

Echeveria plants are typically what most people think of when they hear the word *succulent*. Given enough light, these are wonderful and easy succulents to grow in the home. The native range of *Echeveria* species, in general, includes Texas, Mexico, Central America, and several countries in the western end of South America. The name "hens and chicks" can be misleading; although it is used to sometimes describe echeverias, it is more commonly used—and not to be confused with—the *Sempervivum* genus, which are the hardy cousins of *Echeveria*.

LIGHT: Give your echeverias as much direct sun as you can indoors and place them immediately in front of your brightest window. You may want to avoid these plants if you don't have any bright windows with direct sun. You will likely be disappointed and they will stretch out over time, losing their compact rosette shape.

Echeveria 'Hercules' flowers

POTTING MIX: I like to use a 50/50 mix of succulent/cactus potting mix and ¼-inch pumice.

WATERING: Allow the potting mix to dry out just about completely before watering again.

PROPAGATION: Propagate with leaf cuttings. Pull them off the plant and let them

Echeveria 'Hercules'

air-dry for a couple of days or so in order for the cut to callous over. Then simply lay them flat on a pot of soil. The leaves will start to grow roots and then small pups. Once you see some roots growing, just barely insert the end with roots into the potting mix. Keep the mix barely moist, as this will encourage growth. This is important for very small succulent plants as they're starting to grow. You can also propagate by completely beheading the rosette if it has gotten tall and leggy. Simply let the cut callous over for a couple of days, and then insert it directly into a moist potting mix.

TIPS:

- Succulents are known to be tough plants, but don't take this to mean that they can survive under any conditions. If you don't have enough sun, echeverias will start to stretch out, or etiolate, and their attractive, compact shape will be lost. This will take some time to happen, but it will happen without sufficient light. Always keep sun-loving plants as close to a window as possible.

- Don't make the mistake of adding a miniscule amount of water just because this is a succulent. Succulents need to be watered thoroughly just like any other plant. If you have had issues with rotting, it is likely that you are you not providing enough light, or perhaps you have a pot that's much too big, or other factors are at work.

JADE PLANT
(*Crassula ovata*)

Native to parts of Mozambique and South Africa, this popular succulent does best in bright light, isn't fazed by a little neglect, and doesn't care at all if you have low humidity.

LIGHT: Give your jade plant the brightest window that you can indoors. These are sun loving plants, and although they will grow in windows with no direct sun, the resulting growth will be less compact and more stretched out. If you can, provide them with a bare minimum of two to three hours of direct sun per day.

POTTING MIX: I like to use two parts of a succulent/cactus mix with one part ¼-inch pumice. Jades need rapid drainage and a potting mix that dries out fairly rapidly.

WATERING: Allow at least the top half of the potting mix to dry out before watering again.

PROPAGATION: Jades are easily propagated by leaf cuttings or small stem cuttings. See page 112 for an illustrated guide for jade plant leaf propagation. For a stem cutting, simply cut a small stem (sometimes you will even see aerial roots forming on the plant), allow it to callous over for a couple of days, and then insert it into a moist potting mix.

TIPS:

- Don't be afraid to lightly prune your plant, especially if you want a more compact plant. Remember that if your plant's growth is weak and not compact, you'll have to increase the light it is receiving. Giving it a light pruning and increasing light will result in a sturdier plant.

- When your jades are receiving a lot of direct sun, you may see some of the leaf edges turn reddish. This is perfectly normal and is no cause for alarm.

- If your jade is in a lot of direct sun, it will dry out much more quickly than if it is in lower light. Plants in brighter light will require more frequent watering, even succulents! If you notice that its leaves are starting to wrinkle, feel the potting mix. Chances are it is dry.

A flowering jade plant.

GESNERIACEAE FAMILY OF PLANTS (GESNERIADS)

There are so many delightful members of the gesneriad plant family that you don't have to be limited to the most popular gesneriad of all, the African violet. Most plants in this family are typically grown for their beautiful flowers, and in general, they will thrive in average indoor conditions. In this section, I discuss the care of *Episcia* 'Strawberry Patch' (flame violet) and *Aeschynanthus radicans* (lipstick plant).

Some other members of the gesneriad family that may interest you include *Columnea* (goldfish plant), *Streptocarpus* (cape primrose), and of course *Saintpaulia* (African violet). If you think the plain old African violet is too boring for you, why not try growing a variegated one?

Episcia 'Strawberry Patch'

FLAME VIOLET (*Episcia* spp.)

Episcia species are native to southern Mexico and much of tropical South America. They are relatively quick growers. Although these do have pretty flowers that come in different colors, the foliage in many varieties is truly beautiful. If you can grow their African violet relatives well, you may want to try this beautiful gesneriad.

LIGHT: Episcias thrive in the same conditions as African violets. Give them a window that has plenty of bright, indirect light for the most part. Some early morning or late afternoon sun is beneficial, but avoid too much direct sun exposure.

POTTING MIX: Use a light, airy medium such as African violet mix to which you can add some perlite. You can also use three parts of an all-purpose potting mix plus one part perlite.

WATERING: Keep your episcias evenly moist. As soon as the surface becomes dry, it is time to water.

PROPAGATION: Episcias grow numerous stolons, which are simply long runners, and they produce little pups on the stolons. Simply leave the stolon on the plant, pin the pup down in a small pot filled with potting mix, and keep the mix moist until it roots. Once it is rooted and growing, you can detach it from the parent plant by cutting the stolon.

TIPS:

- Episcias come in a huge variety of leaf colors. Of all the ones I've grown, my favorite is *Episcia* 'Strawberry Patch' with its gorgeous, quilted pink leaves.

- Keep these plants in smaller pots and don't rush to repot. Avoid overpotting these plants, because doing so will increase the risk of the potting mix staying too wet and create the potential for rotting.

- Try not to allow your potting mix to dry out completely. You will quickly get into a situation where many of the lower leaves turn brown and crispy if you are aren't attentive to watering. Consistently moist potting mix is important for keeping these plants in prime condition. These are not plants that you can neglect.

- Grooming is an important task for episcias. Routinely remove any dead or brown leaves. You may also want to cut off the stolons, as this can encourage your plant to bloom. If you do want to keep one or two stolons for the purposes of propagation, leave those and cut off the rest if you want more flowers on your plants. Trimming the stolons will also help keep the plant more compact and not as straggly.

- Episcias do like higher humidity, so be sure to increase your indoor humidity for best results.

Episcia 'Strawberry Patch'

A blooming lipstick plant.

LIPSTICK PLANT
(*Aeschynanthus radicans*)

Native to Thailand and Malaysia. This beautiful cousin of the African violet has a cascading habit that makes it perfect for hanging baskets. The glossy leaves are beautiful in their own right, but the unusual flowers are truly stunning and resemble lipstick tubes. Strict attention to good light, warmth, and an evenly moist potting mix is required for best growth and abundant flowering. This is not a plant that tolerates neglect well.

LIGHT: Without enough light, these plants simply will not flower. Be sure you put them by a nice, bright window. A few hours of direct sun (east or west windows) should do the trick.

POTTING MIX: You can use an African violet potting mix with some added perlite, or simply three parts of an all-purpose potting mix and one part perlite.

WATERING: Consistent moisture is very important for keeping these plants in good shape. Allow the top inch or so of the potting mix to dry out, and then water.

PROPAGATION: The easiest way I've found is to take small stem cuttings and remove the bottom leaves. Insert the cuttings in water until the roots are about an inch long and pot them up.

TIPS:

- There are many varieties to explore, including ones with curly leaves as well as variegated varieties. Flowers come in red and even yellow.
- Leaf and flower drop is a common issue with these plants if it doesn't like your conditions. Never allow your plants to dry out completely. They also despise cold temperatures, so if you have any drafty rooms or your home is not too warm, you may want to avoid this plant.
- If your plant is growing and looks good but hasn't flowered, increase the light levels. When they are happy, they can bloom multiple times per year.
- These plants love humidity. If your plant has suffered a bit from neglect and you want to completely revive it, move it to a shady spot outdoors for the summer. Warm temperatures and humid conditions will completely revitalize this plant, and a summer outdoors will truly do wonders for its growth. I've done this with my plant, and the transformation is truly shocking!
- If your plant has lost many leaves along the vines, don't be afraid to prune off those vines. Your plant will continually produce new growth, even from the base of the plant.

ORCHIDACEAE FAMILY OF PLANTS (ORCHIDS)

Few plants in history have garnered more attention and drama than orchids. Their fabled history, which includes dangerous plant hunting expeditions, greenhouse raids by government officials, and orchid smugglers, have created a mystique unlike any other plant family on Earth.

When many people think of orchids, the common *Phalaenopsis* (moth orchid) comes to mind, but this is an extremely large plant family and there are orchids native to every single continent except for Antarctica. Orchids continue to win our hearts and pique our interest with their exotic flowers and often intoxicating fragrance.

Many orchids are epiphytic (they grow on trees in nature), and they are commonly grown indoors in either a bark mix or sphagnum moss. Because of this, their care must be treated a little differently.

In this section, I share some tips on growing some of my favorites that are also great beginner orchids: the lady of the night (*Brassavola nodosa),* the jewel orchid (*Ludisia discolor*), the lady's slipper orchid (*Paphiopedilum*), the moth orchid (*Phalaenopsis*), and the vanilla orchid (*Vanilla planifolia*). Beware, though, because once the orchid bug bites, there may be no turning back.

A yellow-flowered *Phalaenopsis* orchid.

JEWEL ORCHID
(*Ludisia discolor*)

Native to South China, Sumatra, and the Philippines. This is a great beginner orchid because the potting mix and care are more similar to typical houseplants. Among one of the best lower-light orchids, this plant doesn't seem to mind the low humidity of the average home.

LIGHT: These are among the least demanding orchids in many ways, including light. They are lower-light orchids, but still need sufficient light to grow vigorously and flower. If you have had success with *Phalaenopsis* orchids blooming, great; these plants thrive in the same lighting conditions. My jewel orchid grows directly in front of an eastern-facing window. If you have any really sunny windows (unobstructed south windows in the Northern Hemisphere, or north in the Southern Hemisphere), you should diffuse the light with a sheer curtain or set the plant back so it doesn't get too much, as these orchids don't want to be sitting in sun all day.

POTTING MIX: Unlike many orchids that we grow in our home, these plants are terrestrial and not epiphytes. I grow mine in plain potting mix with some perlite added to it, just like most of my tropical plants. I simply use three parts all-purpose potting mix with one part perlite.

WATERING: Never allow the potting mix to become completely dry. Water when the surface of the potting mix is dry to the touch.

PROPAGATION: You can easily propagate the stems in water. Take stem-tip cuttings and cut just below a node (where the leaf meets the stem). Place the cutting in a jar of water until the roots grow about half an inch long, and then go ahead and pot up the cuttings. You can also place the cuttings directly into moist potting mix to root if you prefer.

TIPS:

- If you see the lower leaves on this plant wilting and turning a lighter reddish or even orange color, it's likely due to potting mix that has dried out completely.
- Although I do run a humidifier to increase the humidity in my sunroom where I keep my *Ludisia discolor*, I have grown it without any measures to increase humidity and experienced no issues at all. Proper watering practices and attention to soil moisture is much more important than worrying about humidity. If you have both, that is a bonus.
- The fleshy stems can be pretty brittle, especially ones that hang over the pot, so be careful when moving them. If they break, you can easily propagate them.
- These orchids are grown mainly for their foliage. They do flower, but it's insignificant. My plant usually flowers in late autumn and winter.

LADY OF THE NIGHT
(*Brassavola nodosa*)

Native to Mexico, Central America, and northern regions of South America. This is a wonderful and easy epiphytic orchid to grow if you have plenty of light. Over time, the plant will reward you with numerous flowers that often perfume the entire room at nighttime. In fact, I can smell my plant even in the adjacent room when it is blooming! This plant will tolerate some neglect, but more consistent care will produce better results.

LIGHT: These orchids need higher light to perform their best and to reward you with flowers. Give your plant the sunniest window that you have. If you don't have much direct sun, or a good grow light, it would probably be best to avoid this orchid because it won't bloom without sufficiently strong light.

POTTING MIX: Any good medium-grade orchid bark mix will be sufficient.

WATERING: Allow your potting mix to dry out almost completely before thoroughly soaking. My own plant is growing in a wooden orchid basket with open slats on the sides and the bottom. If you have these plants mounted, or if you're growing in an open basket like I do, then know that they tend to dry out very quickly and will need more frequent watering than you'd think.

PROPAGATION: You can divide these orchids in the spring.

TIPS:

- All orchids benefit from a summer spent outdoors, and this one is no exception. I place mine outdoors every summer. If you bring it outdoors, be sure to acclimate it carefully to the brighter light. Place it in full shade initially, and gradually increase the sun exposure in order to prevent burning.
- In between watering, mist any exposed roots every day or two to keep them plump and to prevent them from shriveling up.

LADY'S SLIPPER ORCHID (*Paphiopedilum* spp.)

Native to South China and much of tropical Asia. Unlike many orchids, these mostly grow on the forest floor and sometimes on cliffs in pockets of humus. The flowers have an unusual lip that is shaped like a pouch, thus the common name slipper orchid. They will add a bit of intrigue to any houseplant collection!

LIGHT: *Paphiopedilum* are among the best low-light orchids. If you have a spot where moth orchids (*Phalaenopsis*) are growing and blooming for you, it is usually a great location for *Paphiopedilum* as well. Eastern-facing windows would provide a great exposure for these orchids. These are not orchids that want to be in direct sun all day, so you can diffuse any excess sun with a sheer curtain or blinds. Even unobstructed northern-facing windows (in the Northern Hemisphere) or southern-facing windows (in the Southern Hemisphere) that have no direct light can be enough for these plants, but they need to be directly in front of the window.

POTTING MIX: These are commonly grown in either a fine grade fir bark or in pure sphagnum moss. My own plant is growing in pure sphagnum moss and that's what I continue to grow it in since this was the media used when I purchased it.

WATERING: If your plant is growing in pure sphagnum moss, water when the surface of the moss feels dry to the touch. If you have your plant in a bark mix, it will likely dry out more quickly and need more frequent watering. Water when it feels just slightly damp about an inch down. Regardless what mix you use, never allow it to dry out completely, but do allow the surface to dry out.

PROPAGATION: You can easily divide your plants once it has multiple growths. Simply wait until the plant is out of bloom, take the plant out of its pot, and divide it at the roots.

TIPS:

- *Paphiopedilum* plants lack the stiff, thick leaves that many epiphytic orchids have and do not have pseudobulbs, so these don't tolerate drought well.
- If you've had your plant for over a year and it has not rebloomed for you, increase the light.
- You can tell if your *Paphiopedilum* is receiving too much direct sun if the edges are turning a reddish color.
- With consistent care and age, you will get a gorgeous specimen that will grow multiple flowers. I have a specimen that I've had for several years and it grew four flowers during its blooming season. Your plant should continually create new growths at the base, and each new growth will have only one flowering period. The more growths your plant has, the stronger it will become, and the more flowers it will produce.

(CONTINUED)

- In general, *Paphiopedilums* with mottled leaves are warmer growing and work nicely in most homes. The plain green varieties typically are cooler growing and may pose more of a challenge in some home environments.
- If you are beginning with *Paphiopedilums*, try a Maudiae-type *Paphiopedilum*. This type is easily grown in average home conditions, has beautifully mottled foliage, and is attractive even when not in bloom!
- *Paphiopedilums* are very sensitive to salts, so periodically flush your pot with plain water to remove any built-up fertilizer salts. Many growers prefer using rainwater for their plants. I've been using tap water with no issues.
- Airflow is important for orchids. Gently moving the air with a small fan, or even a ceiling fan set on low, is very beneficial for the health of your plants and will help prevent fungal issues.

MOTH ORCHID
(*Phalaenopsis* spp.)

Native to tropical and subtropical Asia as well as Northeast Australia. There are many species of this orchid and they range in habitat from perpetually warm and humid to seasonally dry and cool. This plant is how my orchid obsession started . . . so once you get comfortable with these, beware! The orchid family is very large and there are people who dedicate their lives to just growing various orchids.

LIGHT: *Phalaenopsis* orchids are among the lower-light orchids, but they still absolutely need to be right in front of an appropriate window for good growth and for flowering to occur. If you have a window that gets a couple of hours of direct sun each day, your *Phalaenopsis* should grow nicely. Avoid all-day direct sun, as it is much too bright for these plants. Eastern or western windows would work well.

POTTING MIX: These are typically grown in an orchid bark mix or in pure sphagnum moss. I personally prefer bark mix because I find that sphagnum moss (especially if it's packed in too tightly), takes too long to dry out. You can add some sphagnum moss to your bark mix if pure bark mix dries out too quickly for you.

WATERING: Allow your potting mix to almost completely dry out before watering again. If your plant is growing in sphagnum moss, simply feel the moss. Water when it is almost completely dry. If your plant is growing in a bark mix, you can water in

one of two ways. The first way is to simply take it to your sink, water it like you would any other plant, and let it drain. The second way is what I prefer because it provides a deeper watering. All of my *Phalaenopsis* orchids grow in a pot with a drainage hole, but they are slipped into a cachepot (decorative pot with no hole). I leave the plant in the cachepot, fill it will water, and let it soak for one to two hours. Then I lift the plant out, discard the excess water, place it back in the cachepot, and back to the window it goes.

PROPAGATION: *Phalaenopsis* will occasionally produce a keiki (Hawaiian for "baby" or "child") right on the flower spike. After it grows a bit and has at least a few roots, simply cut it off and pot it up separately.

TIPS:

- Do not use potting soil for these plants, as you will quickly kill them. Although there are some epiphytic plants that can grow in a potting soil mix, this is *not* one of them. If you find that a potting mix of just orchid bark dries out too quickly in your conditions, you can mix in some sphagnum moss. It will retain moisture a little more.

- How do you tell the difference between an aerial root and a flower spike? Roots will be uniformly round at the tip, whereas flower spikes typically will be almost in a mitten shape.

(CONTINUED)

A pink-flowered *Phalaenopsis* orchid.

- *Phalaenopsis* don't have any water-storing pseudobulbs like many other orchids, so they should never stay completely dry for too long. Pseudobulbs are simply bulbous enlargements of the stem. Phalaenopsis also don't have too many leaves to begin with, so careful attention to watering is very important.
- Don't turn your plant when it is growing a flower spike. Keep the orientation with respect to a window so that the flower spike doesn't grow crooked.
- When your plant has lost all of its flowers, cut the flower spike right below where the bottom flower was. Oftentimes, new flower spikes will grow out of the nodes on the flower spike. You can greatly extend the flowering period this way. I never cut off the entire flower spike until it turns brown. New spikes should grow yearly.
- If your plant is not blooming (they normally grow a flower spike in late fall or winter, but can appear at other times of year too), the reason is probably insufficient light. Another way to encourage blooming is to give your plants about a two-week period of cooler night temperatures (55–60 degrees Fahrenheit or so).
- Mist the exposed roots. If your orchid is growing aerial roots, there is nothing at all wrong with this. You can eventually tuck them into your potting mix when you repot them, but in the meantime you should mist the exposed roots. Exposed aerial roots will dry out pretty quickly, especially if you have a low humidity environment. Misting them a couple of times a week in between watering will suffice. You can even do it daily.
- As opposed to watering schedules as I am, I find that most of my *Phalaenopsis* orchids that are growing in just bark mix can be placed on a watering schedule. Once a week works well for me. The reason is that it is pretty difficult to overwater something that's growing in a chunky bark mix.
- Avoid standing water in the crown of the plant. If it sits for too long, it could cause your plant to rot.
- If the plant's leaves are turning reddish along the edges, it could mean that your plant is on the edge of its sun tolerance.
- Last but not least, do not water with ice! This is a marketing gimmick and makes absolutely no sense. These are tropical plants and have no exposure to cold temperatures, let alone ice. I like to tell people that unless you see a monkey with a Popsicle, don't water with ice.

VANILLA ORCHID
(*Vanilla planifolia*)

Native to parts of Mexico, Central America, and Colombia. The vanilla orchid is the source of the prized vanilla beans that are used to flavor so many of our baked goods. These beans are also added as an ingredient to many perfumes. Although easy to grow, this rambling vine needs plenty of space and support.

LIGHT: Vanilla orchids need plenty of light in order for good growth to occur and eventually to flower, so it is important to provide them with a handful of hours of direct sun. Avoid midday sun, as this can be too strong.

POTTING MIX: There are a staggering array of potting mixes that people use to grow this orchid. The important thing is to make sure your combination allows the mix to dry out pretty quickly. I have my plant growing in a terra cotta pot with a growing mix of equal parts all-purpose potting mix, perlite, and orchid bark. Some people grow in pure sphagnum, others in pure orchid bark, and many use variations in between.

WATERING: I allow my potting mix to dry out almost completely, and then I give it a good thorough watering.

PROPAGATION: Take cuttings of the vine and place them right on top of a pot with moist sphagnum moss. Don't pack the moss down too much. You can pin the vine down for proper contact with the moss using U-shaped clips. You can also take a paper clip, bend it into a U-shape, and insert it right over the cutting so that it has contact with the sphagnum moss. Lay the cutting so that any aerial roots have been inserted into the sphagnum moss. Maintain warm temperatures and high humidity for best results. New growth will start to occur at the nodes. Avoid burying the cut end of the cutting into the moss to prevent rotting.

TIPS:

- Mist the aerial roots regularly to provide moisture.
- These plants prefer warm, humid conditions for best growth.
- Vanilla orchids need a support to climb on. I inserted three 6-foot bamboo stakes in the terra cotta pot that I have my plant growing in and tied the stakes on top to create a tripod. If you do the same, simply secure the vines to the stakes with twine or twist ties. Eventually, the plant will wrap its aerial roots around the stakes. Once it reaches the top, you can train it back down to the surface of the potting mix if you'd like, and then back up. These plants can grow tremendously long. You can also use a rough slab of wood as a support.
- If you take any cuttings or accidentally break the plant, promptly wash your hands to remove any skin irritants.

(CONTINUED)

My vanilla orchid growing on bamboo support stakes.

- Upon the recommendation of an expert vanilla orchid grower, I broke my general rule of thumb for this plant as far as going up only one pot size when repotting. I moved it from a 4-inch pot to a 10-inch pot. I felt comfortable doing this for two reasons: I used a terra cotta pot and I have the plant growing in a very chunky mixture so it will dry out quickly. The growth of the plant really took off once I placed it in a larger pot and gave it support stakes.

- Flowering will take a while to occur indoors, and when it does, the flowers last only one day. Part of the reason why vanilla beans and vanilla extract are so expensive is that the process is all very labor-intensive. All flowers are hand-pollinated, and given that the flowers last only a day, everything requires close monitoring. Under good conditions, once your plant is a few years old, you may try and coax flowering to occur by pruning the tips off the vine.

OTHER PLANT FAMILIES

Last but not least are a variety of popular houseplants. I have only one plant representing each of the remaining plant families that I chose to include in this book, so I grouped them all together here. The following plants are discussed: aloe (*Aloe* spp.), Polka dot begonia (*Begonia maculata* 'Wightii'), parlor palm (*Chamaedorea elegans*), rattlesnake plant (*Goeppertia insignis*), rubber plant (*Ficus elastica*), purple shamrock plant (*Oxalis triangularis*), Chinese money plant, or UFO plant (*Pilea peperomioides*), and string of pearls (*Curio rowleyanus*).

Healthy aloe growing next to a bright window.

ALOE (*Aloe* spp.)

Aloe species are native to much of Africa, as well as Madagascar, Jordan, and the Arabian Peninsula. These are great plants to acquire if you have sunny windows. In addition, they tolerate neglect well and do not need any special attention paid to humidity.

FAMILY: Asphodelaceae

LIGHT: These are sun-loving plants, so place them right in front of the brightest window that you have. They love direct sun. You can grow them in front of windows that don't have any direct sun, but the growth won't be as compact and it will be weaker.

POTTING MIX: I use two parts cactus/succulent potting mix with one part ¼-inch pumice and one part perlite. It is a rapidly draining mix and doesn't hold on to too much moisture. This is a great potting mix for succulents in general.

WATERING: Water when the potting mix is completely dry.

PROPAGATION: Aloe plants are so easy to propagate from offsets or pups that grow at the base of the mother plant. Simply separate the pup by gently twisting away from the mother plant, let the pup air-dry for a day or two, and pot it directly into a small pot with the indicated potting mix. Water well, then wait until the mix is mostly dry before watering again.

TIPS:

- Don't overpot aloe, otherwise the potting mix may stay too wet for too long and this will encourage root rot. If it needs to be repotted, only increase the pot size by one size. For example, you can go from a 4-inch pot to a 6-inch pot, but *no bigger.*

- If you are seeking to place your plant in a higher light position, make sure you slowly acclimate your plant to higher light or it will burn. If you've burned your plant, don't mistake this for aloe not liking full sun. *You simply haven't acclimated it slowly enough to higher light.*

- Terra cotta pots work very well with aloes since the potting mix will dry out more quickly, which succulents need. Terra cotta will also anchor the plant down since they become top heavy over time.

CHINESE MONEY PLANT, OR UFO PLANT
(*Pilea peperomioides*)

Native to China. Also known as the Chinese money plant or UFO plant, this delightful plant has taken the world by storm. Once hard to find and expensive, it is now very common. It can be tricky to grow well, but once you get the hang of it, it is sure to be a delight. This is not a plant for the neglectful indoor gardener.

FAMILY: Urticaceae

LIGHT: In order to truly have a beautiful specimen, you must make light a top priority. I have my plants in front of an eastern-facing window. These plants can take quite a bit of direct sun, contrary to what you may have read elsewhere. I would recommend a location directly in front of a window that gets two to four hours of sun in the morning or late afternoon.

POTTING MIX: I've been using two parts all-purpose potting mix plus one part ¼-inch pumice. Many mixes work well as long as you amend them to increase porosity of the mix.

WATERING: I've found that there is a pretty delicate balance with this plant as far as potting mix moisture goes. I try to allow only the top inch or so to dry out before watering thoroughly again.

PROPAGATION: These plants propagate very readily since they produce a lot of pups or offsets. If you have a leggy plant, you can chop off the stem, place it in water to root, then pot it up. Similarly, you can separate the small pups at the base of the plant. If you can get a bit of the root system, pot them up right away in small pots. If it's too difficult to separate any of them, you can simply cut them as close to the surface of the pot as you can, root them in water, and then plant in a small pot.

TIPS:

- Be sure to turn your plants often in order to encourage even growth. I normally turn my plant 180 degrees once a week.
- This is not a plant you can ignore. Very consistent care is needed to grow a beautiful specimen.
- Never allow your potting mix to dry out completely. You will rapidly lose many of the lower leaves if you do this. They may turn yellow or brown and proceed to fall off. Similarly, never allow your plant to sit in water at all. Always discard excess water.
- If you have had your plant for at least several months and find that your plant is not growing, or not growing any pups, increase your light. This is not a plant like pothos or peace lilies that can withstand dim conditions. You will be disappointed if you don't provide enough light.
- Curling or cupping leaves is caused by improper watering and/or poor attention to soil moisture. *First make sure that you have your plant right in front of an appropriate window. Without this, you will not achieve the results you're looking for.* Review my tips for watering in Key 4 (page 50).

Chinese money plants, also known as UFO plants (*Pilea peperomioides*).

- Do *not* overpot this plant. Some plants are forgiving of this, but this plant is not one of them. Only repot if it is root-bound and you're having to water very frequently as a result. When you do repot, only go up one pot size, for example, from a 4-inch pot to a 6-inch pot. Do *not* go larger than that! I've done this out of laziness in the past (I didn't have an appropriately sized pot), and I had to repot it again after I purchased a pot in the size I needed. Upsizing to a pot that is too large may cause the potting mix to take much too long to dry out, and as a result you may notice all sorts of issues with leaves not flattening out, or worse yet, root rot. This will be especially problematic if you have your plant

in low light and with low-porosity potting mix.
- You may find little hard specs scattered on the undersides of the leaves that look like little grains of salt. Reportedly, these are mineral deposits that the plant is excreting. I use tap water to water all my plants, so I observe these specs on my plant, but they do not harm the plant.
- Don't freak out over every yellow leaf. Even with proper attention to care, you will still occasionally get a yellow or brown leaf or two. Accept it as a part of the natural growth cycle. I find that this can especially occur in the wintertime when light levels are much lower. You can choose to move your plant to a brighter location during the winter.

PARLOR PALM
(Chamaedorea elegans)

Native to much of Mexico as well as Belize, Guatemala, and Honduras. This is the only palm that I grow indoors because I think it is the easiest one by far to grow and it stays a manageable size, unlike many other palms, even after many years. Like many palms, they enjoy higher humidity, but as long as you give them proper attention to watering, it's not a strict requirement.

FAMILY: Arecaceae

LIGHT: This plant will tolerate quite low light, and I've even grown it in office settings with no windows but with fluorescent lights on all day. Don't expect wonderful growth in these conditions, though. Best growth is achieved if you place it right in front of a window that receives bright but indirect light. They can easily take a few hours of direct sun. Eastern or western windows are ideal, but avoid full sun all day long.

POTTING MIX: Any good all-purpose potting mix, with additional perlite added (3:1 ratio) is great.

WATERING: Allow the top quarter of the potting mix to dry out, and then water thoroughly. Avoid allowing the potting mix to dry out completely. Do this repeatedly and you will rapidly get multiple browning fronds, ugly brown tips, and fronds that struggle to open properly.

PROPAGATION: The easiest way to propagate these is by division. Often, when you purchase a small plant at a shop, there are several plants in the same pot. Simply divide them at the roots and pot them up if you wish to make more plants.

TIPS:

- Parlor palms are fairly shallow rooted, so avoid unusually deep pots.
- If your plant is happy and mature enough, it will often reward you with regular sprays of yellow flowers. This can be both a blessing and a curse because the little yellow "balls" will drop to the floor and cause a mess. I normally cut off the flower sprays when I first see them appear.
- Although high humidity will be beneficial, if you maintain consistent soil moisture, your plant will be just fine with average indoor humidity.
- Palms are prone to spider mites indoors. Regular misting or rinsing of the leaves in a sink or shower is a good way to deter them.

My flowering *Begonia maculata*.

POLKA DOT BEGONIA
(*Begonia maculata 'Wightii'*)

This stunning, relatively quick-growing begonia with white polka dot foliage is a native of southeast Brazil. As a bonus, they grow beautiful clusters of numerous, white flowers. This is not a plant that tolerates neglect well, as begonias are quite particular with soil moisture and detest drying out too much.

FAMILY: Begoniaceae

LIGHT: For best growth indoors, give this plant at least a couple of hours of direct sun. Placement directly in front of a window with an eastern or western exposure is ideal.

POTTING MIX: I use a potting mix of three parts all-purpose potting mix with one part perlite.

WATERING: I've found that begonias are not forgiving at all with neglect. They detest their potting mix going completely dry. Allow no more than the top quarter of the potting mix to dry out before watering thoroughly again.

PROPAGATION: Propagate by snipping off canes. You'll want to make sure you have one or two nodes on the cane. Simply place them in water. Once the roots are about an inch long at the most, go ahead and pot them up. They root easily from cuttings.

TIPS:

- If you have inconsistent conditions, such as erratic watering, this plant is prone to leaf drop.
- If your plant has gotten too leggy or has sparse foliage, give it a good pruning. These plants respond very well to hard pruning, and I've rejuvenated my plant by cutting the canes back to three or four nodes. They will flush out in new growth in no time and you'll have a brand new plant. You can use the parts that you trimmed off for propagation.
- If you keep the potting mix too dry, brown leaf tips can quickly occur.
- Begonias in general love higher humidity, but be sure to also try and provide good air circulation in order to prevent powdery mildew, which begonias can be prone to.

PURPLE SHAMROCK PLANT (*Oxalis triangularis*)

Native to much of South America, the striking purple foliage of this plant makes a grand statement. It is easy to grow as well! The leaves and flowers close at night and open back up during the day, making this plant a wonderful subject for time-lapse videos.

FAMILY: Oxalidaceae

LIGHT: Indoors, these plants need at least two or three hours of direct sun each day to look their best. If your plants are leggy or sparse, and not full, chances are that you're not giving it enough light.

POTTING MIX: An all-purpose potting mix with some perlite added (three parts to one part) is a great mix.

WATERING: These plants like to stay slightly moist, but allow the top inch of the potting mix to dry out before watering again.

PROPAGATION: These plants grow from corms, which resemble small pine cones. As a result, this plant is easily propagated by division. This is most easily done while the plant is dormant. Once the foliage has died back, take the corms out of the pot and divide them up into as many pots as you'd like.

TIPS:

- These plants are hardy down to USDA Zone 6, so many people grow these in the garden outdoors.
- I like to bring my plant outdoors when the weather gets warm in the springtime and leave it outside until about October or November, before temperatures go down to freezing. At that point, I stop watering, place it in a cool, dark place (as long as temperatures are above freezing) for a few weeks. The foliage will all die back. After about four to six weeks of dormancy, I remove all the dead foliage and bring it back to its growing location indoors to start growth back up again. You don't have to force dormancy every year, but just be aware that your plant may go dormant on its own every so often. If this happens, give it a rest period as described here and then resume normal care.
- If you start this plant from bare corms, don't be afraid to plant several in the same pot so that you have a nice, full plant. Plant the corms no more than an inch apart.

RATTLESNAKE PLANT
(*Goeppertia insignis*)

Previously known as *Calathea lancifolia*, this native of Brazil has striking foliage and is perhaps the "easiest" of the *Goeppertia* species to grow indoors, though it is not a plant that will tolerate neglect. As a member of the prayer plant family, the leaves fold up at night and then settle back down during the daytime.

FAMILY: Marantaceae

LIGHT: My plant is perfectly happy right in front of an eastern-facing window where it gets some morning sun. Providing two to three hours of direct sun in early morning or late afternoon is ideal. Avoid midday sun, as it is likely to be too strong for these plants. Windows with no direct sun at all are also good, but keep it right in front of the window for best growth.

POTTING MIX: Using three parts all-purpose potting mix plus one part perlite does the trick for me.

WATERING: Aim to keep your plant pretty evenly moist. As soon as the surface is dry to the touch, water.

PROPAGATION: You can propagate this plant very easily by division.

TIPS:

- Rattlesnake plant, like any plant in the *Goeppertia* genus, are not the easiest plants to manage indoors. They require *consistent* care and attention. Warmth, high humidity, proper light, and good watering practices are essential. Unfortunately, these conditions are hard to achieve indoors without deliberate effort.

- Crispy, brown edges on leaves are often the result of dry potting mix. Never allow your potting mix to dry out completely. The quickest way to produce a horrendous-looking *Goeppertia* is to let the potting mix dry out too much. Do this repeatedly, and you will have a very brown, crispy plant.

- These plants are reportedly sensitive to salts in tap water, so many people use distilled water with good results. Rain water probably is better. I personally use tap water because I have too many plants to fuss with, and I am fine living with the occasional brown tips on leaves. More dramatic brown edges result from keeping the potting mix too dry.

- High humidity is preferred, so be sure to run a humidifier if your indoor air is dry, especially in the wintertime if you use forced air heat.

RUBBER PLANT
(*Ficus elastica*)

Native to Nepal, China, Malaysia, and surrounding regions. One of the most popular houseplants, and also one of the most poorly cared for, a rubber plant can grow into a beautiful specimen indoors with enough light and consistent care. It's one of the best large houseplants you can grow indoors, and as long as you give them enough light and pay proper attention to watering, you will be successful.

FAMILY: Moraceae

LIGHT: Often labeled as a low-light plant, rubber plants in fact thrive in direct sun. They may tolerate low light for a while, but you will not achieve good growth if you locate them in an area of low light. Keep your rubber plant right in front of a window (any window) for best results. A few hours of sun a day will greatly benefit this plant.

POTTING MIX: My own large plant has been growing in a mixture of all-purpose potting mix, perlite, and orchid bark for many years. I used roughly three parts all-purpose potting mix, one part perlite, and one part orchid bark.

WATERING: Allow about the top quarter of the potting mix to dry out, and then water thoroughly.

PROPAGATION: Because of the thick, woody stems, propagation is best done by air layering. In a nutshell, you simply wound the stem, wrap it with moist sphagnum moss, wrap it in plastic, and wait for

As evidenced by my rubber plant, these plants can grow very large in the home.

rooting to occur. It takes a few months, but this method will result in a lot less stress on the plant.

TIPS:

- Try and place your plant in a warm, bright location that doesn't receive any cold or hot drafts. *Ficus* in general hate drafts.
- The broad leaves will collect a lot of dust, so be sure to take a damp sponge and gently clean off the

leaves. Avoid any leaf-shine products, as they are not necessary.

- If your plant is not growing, move it to a brighter location. Another common complaint is that newer leaves are smaller than previous leaves. Remember that our conditions at home are much less ideal than those of the greenhouses where they were first grown, so this is one reason why this is occurring. Give your plant as much light as you can indoors for best results.

- One word of caution: If you have your plant in a darker location and you are moving it to a much sun-nier location, you should gradually increase the amount of direct sun. Even though these plants can take plenty of direct sun indoors, you must acclimate your plant slowly so that it doesn't burn.

- The same recommended cultural conditions described here also apply for fiddle-leaf fig (*Ficus lyrata*). In all my experiences with helping people with this plant, the two most common pitfalls are not enough light and/or improper watering. Give this plant the brightest location that you can and follow proper watering practices described in Key 4 (page 50).

STRING OF PEARLS
(*Curio rowleyanus*)

Native to South Africa. Most sources list this plant as *Senecio rowleyanus*, but you'll also find it listed it as *Curio rowleyanus*. This beautiful trailing succulent will reward you with dainty and fragrant flowers if you provide it with suitable growing conditions. If you can't provide sufficient light, this plant can be notoriously difficult to grow.

FAMILY: Asteraceae

LIGHT: The key for growing string of pearls successfully indoors is to provide it with as much direct sun as you can. If you don't have any particularly sunny windows, place it right under a grow light. I wasn't able to successfully grow this plant for the long term until I invested in a suitable grow light, because we don't have any particularly sunny windows. If you can provide enough light, this can be a pretty carefree plant!

POTTING MIX: A very sharply draining potting mix is very important for this succulent. I like to use one part succulent/cactus potting mix and one part ¼-inch pumice.

WATERING: I thoroughly soak every time I water, and then I allow the potting mix to go completely dry in between. Don't wait too long though, otherwise the "pearls" will shrivel. Some shriveling is okay, but be sure to water if you see this *and* you determine that the potting mix is indeed dry.

PROPAGATION: You can easily propagate cuttings either in water or by directly inserting the ends of multiple cuttings into moist potting mix. Simply remove the pearls at the bottom of each cutting and place that portion into water or potting mix. You can also take a long strand and coil it up right on the surface of a pot filled with potting mix. This method will result in a plant that has a fuller crown. Keep the mix relatively moist to encourage root growth, and you can back off on the watering as the plant grows.

TIPS:

- One quick way to kill this plant is to repot it into a pot that is much bigger than the previous pot. Doing so can cause the potting mix to take a long time to dry out, especially if the volume of soil is too big. As a general guideline, only move up one pot size if you need to repot.
- This plant has a pretty shallow root system, so don't use any particularly deep pots, otherwise the potting mix will take longer to dry out.
- If you have struggled with this plant, you will find that string of bananas (*Curio radicans*) is much easier to grow and much less demanding.

index

Page numbers in *italics* indicate illustrations.

about the author

RAFFAELE DI LALLO has been growing houseplants for over 30 years, and it all started in grade school as a way to clean the air from his father's smoking habit. It quickly became an obsession, and he continues to grow a vast array of plants both indoors and out. In 2017, he received a phone call from a friend who suggested that he start a blog, which Raffaele promptly did the next day. There was no looking back, and his Ohio Tropics houseplant care website quickly made it to the top 10 houseplant care blogs on the internet, according to Feedspot.

The blog initially provided information on how to achieve a tropical flair to gardens in cold-weather areas like Ohio. Later on, its main emphasis became houseplant care, which remains the sole focus to this day.

Raffaele received his BS in chemical engineering from Northwestern University in Evanston, Illinois, in 2000. The thinking and questioning skills he developed in his studies, combined with his passion for growing plants, have led him to become a "plant solver." You can source Raffaele's expertise via his virtual and in-person, houseplant consultation business where he helps people work through their houseplant challenges. Contact Raffaele directly through his Ohio Tropics website for any inquiries, or message him on Instagram (@ohiotropics).

Raffaele received his Certificate of Home Horticulture from Oregon State University as a part of their Master Gardener program, completed the Green Gardener program at the Cleveland Botanical Garden, is a member of the American Orchid Society as well as Garden Communicators International, and worked part-time as a freelance writer for the popular Gardening Know How website. He also self-published a succinct but very popular guide to orchid care, *Moth Orchid Mastery*.